FORD TRACTOR
IMPLEMENTS

Chester Peterson Jr. & Rod Beemer

MBI Publishing Company

First published in 1998 by MBI Publishing Company, 729 Prospect Avenue, PO Box 1, Osceola, WI 54020-0001 USA

The information in this book is true and complete to the best of our knowledge. All recommendations are made without any guarantee on the part of the author or Publisher, who also disclaim any liability incurred in connection with the use of this data or specific details.

We recognize that some words, model names, and designations, for example, mentioned herein are the property of the trademark holder. We use them for identification purposes only. This is not an official publication.

MBI Publishing Company books are also available at discounts in bulk quantity for industrial or sales-promotional use. For details write to Special Sales Manager at Motorbooks International Publishers & Wholesalers, 729 Prospect Avenue, PO Box 1, Osceola, WI 54020-0001 USA.

Library of Congress Cataloging-in-Publication Data

Peterson, Chester, Jr.
      Ford tractor implements / Chester
Peterson, Jr. & Rod Beemer.
         p.   cm. -- (Farm tractor color history)
      Includes index.
      ISBN 0-7603-0428-9 (pbk. : alk. paper)
      1. Agricultural implements--History. 2.
Ford tractors--History.
      I. Beemer, Rod, 1941- II. Title. III. Series: Farm
tractor color history.
S676.P465   1998
631.3'72--dc21   98-23726

On the front cover: Farming took a huge leap forward in safety and efficiency with the Ferguson three-point implement system. This rare English-built Type 60-AC Ferguson quarter-turn reversible plow embodies all the qualities of the original Ferguson system. It provides a consistent plowing depth and doesn't put the operator in peril when hitting a buried object.

On the frontispiece: A close-up view of the Type 60-AC "butterfly" as it slices the earth and displaces the dirt in one direction. It's well-suited for hillsides where it's desirable to turn all furrows uphill to combat erosion.

On the title page: Breaking up grassland or sod-bound soils is this Scottish-bottom's specialty.

On the back cover top: This Ferguson-Sherman Four-Row Weeder effectively killed weeds. It accomplished its goal by agitating the topsoil in planted crops, which halted early weed growth before the crops emerged from the soil. The weeder could cover a lot of ground in a hurry because the implement could travel at the tractor's maximum speed. **bottom:** This Type PA 021 Ferguson three-bottom disc plow was made in the early 1950s. The three-bottom design has nonserrated blades, allowing it to mix an abundant amount of surface trash with soil. It can construct and maintain terraces, work heavy or wet soils, and plow fields with a large amount of stones or roots.

Printed in Hong Kong through World Print, Ltd.

Dedication

To Mary Peterson and Dawn Beemer!

Acknowledgments

We, the authors, are gratefully indebted to all the contributors. This book wouldn't have been possible without them. The valuable assistance rendered by these people is herewith gratefully acknowledged:

Our editors, Lee Klancher and Paul Johnson, for their faith in us, which at times exceeded our own.

Restorers, collectors, and others, who provided the subjects for camera and questions, include Roland Bartley, Dave Benson, Roger Cornell, Dwight Emstrom, Howard Howell, Eugene Kruse, John Smith, and Ron Stauffer.

Archivists and research personnel who were helpful and gracious were Darleen Flaherty, Assistant Archivist, Ford Motor Company Archives; Cathleen Latendresse, Linda Skolarus, Terry Hoover, and staff, Henry Ford Museum Research Center, Greenfield Village, Michigan; Linda Johnson and John Skarstad, Special Collections, University of California, Davis; Peter Ledwith, The Farm Museum Archives, Milton, Ontario, Canada; Linda Davis, Salina, Kansas, Public Library; plus many other librarians and historians who sought out requested information for us.

A special thanks to Palmer Fossum, Don Horner, and David Lory for their help, plus Chuck Beemer for his assistance with artwork.

And, to anybody we may have unintentionally omitted, we thank you.

Contents

Foreword

I have had a great interest in the Ford tractor and implement world since 1936 when I started operating a Fordson tractor, and 1940 when my father purchased our first 9N and implements. I have in my personal collection many of the machines that are mentioned in this book. I would truly recommend this book to anyone having interest along these lines. The authors deeply researched the history of each machine, and the function for which each implement was designed in order to produce a book with great detail.

Ford implements are designed to meet the needs of farmers and users in different parts of the country who have different situations and needs such as soil conditions, weed problems, and acreage. Some of the plows, blades, cultivators, and such are of the economy type for the farmer who doesn't need anything elaborate; and other models are more beefy and deluxe for the person who feels more plush in something fancy.

There is a lot of history connected to the development of these machines, and the changes made as the year vintages went along. The Ferguson-Sherman line of implements came first with the 9N and 2N tractors, which were painted mostly battleship grey; Then came the Dearborn line of equipment from 1948 to 1954 vintage, producing the 8N and Jubilee/NAA tractors which were red and light grey. The Dearborn Line was dropped in 1958 and was picked-up by the Ford Script Emblem Line to match the 600-800-900 tractor line and later the 601-801-901 series, which was then followed by the Blue Line of implements.

I think this is a great guide for someone who is choosing implements for a Ford tractor collection. I wish everyone well and good luck in studying the implement specs in this book, and with purchases of the same for your tractor.

–Palmer Fossum

Introduction

Documenting the development of the three-point system of mounted implements can lead you on an interesting journey. It has been for us. Things that are fascinating, however, aren't always clear-cut. Nor is the path invariably straight.

To help you keep your bearings and understand what happened during the three-point revolution and its refinement, a simplified overview is provided.

Harry Ferguson was the father of the three-point system. His three-point concept, initiated in his native Ireland, spread throughout the world. Ferguson System, and later non-Ferguson System, three-point implements were manufactured in several countries, plus there was regular importing and exporting between these countries. Thus, it's obviously impossible to establish all points of origins for the manufacturers of many of these implements.

The three-point system began with Ferguson's design of a mounted plow for the Eros tractor, which was manufactured in Ireland. His second design was fitted to the Fordson tractor and was first manufactured in Ireland. Later it was also built in at least two locations in the United States.

Harry Ferguson's handmade "Black" tractor with internal hydraulics was the foundation of the first true three-point system. This tractor and its implements were built at Ferguson's May Street shop in Belfast, Northern Ireland, in 1933. All subsequent three-point equipment springs from these original Ferguson-designed implements.

Beginning in 1936, implements for the Ferguson-Brown tractor were built by David Brown Tractors, Ltd., Huddersfield, England. But, David Brown production ceased in 1938. Then Harry Ferguson and Henry Ford brought out the N-Series tractor in 1939, along with its line of three-point equipment manufactured in the United States.

However, the first real production of three-point implements began in 1936 at Huddersfield, England, with four pieces of equipment. By 1948, just a dozen years later, the implement family tree included scores of manufacturers in the United States and abroad, bearing a multitude of identifying plates.

In this book you'll find a number of these implements were developed and manufactured by firms that also marketed them under their own company names. In addition, a multitude of manufacturers adapted their equipment for the three-point system or began manufacturing specialty items for the system.

As you would expect, certain implements became highly popular, sometimes with several variants, while others were produced in quite limited volume.

The bottom line: There's just no way a single book on three-point equipment for Ford-Ferguson tractors can include something about every such implement ever offered to farmers.

Some of us didn't realize it at the time, when we drove those first Ford tractors with Ferguson System implements, but we were participants in a milestone in agriculture, arguably the most far-reaching advancement in farming in general and agricultural engineering in particular that the world has ever experienced.

CHAPTER ONE

Ferguson's Quest to Revolutionize Farming

DEVELOPING THE RIGHT IMPLEMENTS

How do you demonstrate—graphically and without any danger—to farmers how the Ferguson three-point system is so much safer than the pull-type plows of the day? Attach the model pull-type plow, hit the "obstruction," and watch the front end of the model tractor rear up, and possibly over. Then put on the model three-point hitch plow, hit the "obstruction," and observe that nothing dangerous happens. This is an original demonstrator tractor with two plows. It's one of only a few left.

djectives to describe Harry Ferguson are many—and almost equally divided between complimentary and otherwise.

Eccentric? Well, the term does crop up every so often in references to Ferguson. For instance, at his Abbottswood estate he continually frustrated his groundskeepers by insisting that the trees grow perfectly straight and that the small lake be kept precisely round.

Perfectionist? Absolutely. Here's just one of many illustrations: The policy at his implement factory was that each bolt was to be lightly oiled before assembly and that exactly the length of two threads were to extend beyond the nut.

One day an employee was assembling an implement for testing purposes, not for sale. He knew that the implement was to be disassembled soon and studied, and that it would never reach a customer. Harry happened by, and, well, the employee was soon taking everything apart and lightly oiling each bolt before reassembling it properly with exactly two threads worth of bolt showing.

Persistent? Without a doubt. "Quit" just wasn't part of Ferguson's vocabulary. He worked—and worked hard—at his dream for 40 years, until it became a worldwide standard for mounted equipment.

A cantankerous, hardheaded, S.O.B.? Some of the time, at least. Henry Ford II diplomatically concluded that Ferguson was "a difficult person to get along with in a business way."

Model 8N Ford tractor and Dearborn plow at one time symbolized the height of effective, efficient farm mechanization.

Regardless of whatever words you use to describe Harry Ferguson, be you admirer or detractor, facts and patents all point to this man as the originator of the first-ever commercially successful three-point system for mounted implements.

Roots in Ireland

Henry George Ferguson was born fourth in a family of 11 children at Lake House, Growell, Dromore, County Down, Ireland, November 4, 1884. Although he always went by the name "Harry," nobody is certain exactly why.

His parents, James and Mary, owned and farmed approximately 100 acres in Ireland. Owning land put his family in a better economic stratum than many rural Irish families of the time. However, it still required sun-up to sun-down toil to provide a "bit-better-than-poverty" existence.

Perhaps the lingering taste of this endless toil during his childhood stimulated the bound-less drive Ferguson had for reforming agriculture through his tractor and machinery inventions. At any rate, he had enough of farming by age 18 to call it quits on both accounts. He resolved to leave family, home, and Ireland, and emigrate to Canada or the United States. His older brother, Joe, had preceded him in leaving home, not to emigrate but to open an auto shop in Belfast.

Joe persuaded his younger brother to apprentice as a mechanic at his auto workshop, a job that also included occasionally driving cars. Harry discovered a love of cars and engines that immediately pushed any thought of Canada or America from his mind.

Those years between 1902 and 1911 whetted Ferguson's appetite for anything mechanical. He raced motorcycles and automobiles and built an airplane that accomplished the first successful flight in Ireland.

Incidentally, Ferguson also designed, built, and flew the first tricycle-gear aircraft. Now almost all new aircraft run on tricycle gear with a nose wheel instead of a tail wheel.

Eventually, the siren song of independence overcame Ferguson's love of racing his brother's cars and flying his own airplane. So, Ferguson left his brother's business in order to launch his own. In 1911, he opened May Street Motors on May Street in Belfast, Ireland.

A year later the business was renamed Harry Ferguson, Ltd. His company took on a number of franchises including, Vauxhall, Maxwell, and Ford automobiles. In 1914, it even began selling

The Origins of Farm Implements

Man first used a pointed stick to poke a depression into the earth and then dropped a seed into the resulting depression. Then a stick or a sharpened piece of bone was used in the form of a crude plow. In the next major evolutionary step, man was replaced by animal as the main power source.

And, not only did an ox, horse, or mule save the farmer undue sweat and time, but the farmer could readily hitch one up to pull a small log that still had several branches attached. This was a significant advancement, because he could prepare considerably more ground—both faster and easier. Crude? Certainly. And farming was still hard, dirty, physical labor.

The Stone, Bronze, and Iron Ages all saw farm implement improvements in increasing numbers and greater complexity. Animal and human muscle still provided the power to operate these vastly improved tools.

However, the planter, the tiller, and the harvester proved that these implements were a better way than previous tools.

R. Douglas Hurt, in his book *American Farm Tools from Hand-Power to Steam-Power*, succinctly summed up the slowly developing better way:

Technological change takes time, and it depends upon three criteria.

First, it requires cumulative knowledge. Before anyone could build a steam engine someone had to invent the wheel. Success in technological innovation depends upon knowledge gained from prior experience. An inventor draws upon the past—accepting, rejecting, and synthesizing—to shape a new idea into a workable product.

Second, technological change relies upon a perceived need. In agriculture, as well as in other endeavors, the new invention must clearly work to the owner's advantage. If nothing is to be gained, such as plowing more easily, reaping more quickly, or threshing more efficiently, there would be no reason to adopt the new invention.

Third, the product of technological innovation must be affordable. If farmers had not had sufficient means to purchase a cast-iron plow, the invention would have never replaced the wooden moldboard.

Then came the dawning of the Industrial Age. About this time, too, the world population pushed itself out of the starting blocks to begin an impressive sprint upward in numbers. And for the first time, more people lived in the world's urban areas than on farms. These combined factors triggered an ever-increasing need for enhanced food production.

In this country, as well as all throughout history in the other parts of the world, there have been fertile plains, rich bottomland, and sometimes marginal upland.

With few exceptions, the first order of business has always been to somehow transform virgin land to cropland. And that task requires a specialized breaking tool, the piece of equipment that's evolved into the modern plow.

Just after the turn of the century the terms "motor plow" or "auto plow" were applied to many new inventions aimed at the agrimarket. Ford Motor Company entered the race as early as 1907 with its experimental Automobile Plow.

Another hopeful was the Hackney Auto Plow of 1911. The Hackney Manufacturing Company was started in 1909 to build iron gates. But, its engineers became infected by the tractor and implement frenzy of the period, and two short years later the firm offered the first of three auto plows. However, a plant fire in 1918 ended its hopes of solving the plowing problems of the world.

John Deere commissioned C. H. Melvin to design a motor plow in 1912. Only one experimental unit was completed, and the project was shelved in 1914. B. F. Avery debuted its Louisville Motor Plow in 1915. The design suggested that it was first and foremost a machine for plowing.

Men like John Deere, Cyrus Hall McCormick, J. I. Case, and many other pioneer agribusiness personalities prevailed and continued to provide products that truly were a better way. Unfortunately, these improved implements were still hitched behind an animal "engine."

Then, with loud rattling of heavy metal, billowing clouds of black smoke, and a piercing steam whistle, the age of mechanical power rolled onto the world's farmlands. It represented sheer genius for the time.

The first steam traction machines were much too massive and too expensive for most small farmers and the generally limited acreages of the era. A typical steam traction engine might weigh anywhere from between 10 to 25 tons and cost in excess of $10,000. Remember that in 1922 a Fordson tractor could be taken home for as little as $395.

These gigantic hunks of metal also had a nasty habit of crashing through road bridges that were designed to handle lighter horse-drawn farm wagons. Oh, yes, there was also the occasional explosion resulting from ill-designed boilers and the limited metallurgy knowledge of early manufacturers.

Again, R. Douglas Hurt said it well:

Several technical problems involving power and weight had to be overcome before a fully satisfactory steam engine could be used for plowing.

The cast-iron gearing of the steam engines designed for threshing were only strong enough to move the tractor from one place to another. Cast-iron gears could not withstand the strain placed upon them during drawbar work.

Also, in order to gain sufficient traction, inventors at first utilized the engine's weight instead of an efficient combination of gears. Although traction could be improved by placing most of the weight above the rear wheels, these steam engines were usually so heavy they bogged down in the field, particularly in damp or soft soil.

Lastly, the plows, harrows, and grain drills on the market were designed for horse power. Horse-drawn implements did not work properly behind steam tractors. Consequently, plowing, seeding, and harvesting operations would not be improved until new implements were developed to work efficiently with the increased draft of a traction steam plowing engine.

Soon a better way was advancing on two fronts. Leading the way was the increasingly more dependable power source that could replace the traditional oxen, horse, and mule. However, if this new power was to be efficiently harnessed, a new generation of farm equipment needed to be created.

It was inevitable that farmers would attempt to modify the horse-drawn equipment they already owned during this transition from animal power to mechanization, so they could hitch up to a steam traction engine or a tractor. This, however, was seldom a marriage made in heaven.

Most such adapted implements usually didn't trail as well behind tractors as they did following draft animals. With animal power, if the implement struck an obstruction, such as a tree stump, the draft animal simply stopped and waited for the boss man to remove the obstacle.

It was different—dangerously different—with tractor power. After striking an obstacle, the torque transferred to the rear drive wheels and there was often a tendency for the entire tractor to rotate around its rear axle—and in many cases flip over backward. Many early tractor operators were seriously injured or killed as a result of this hazard.

Yet another consideration was that with horse-drawn equipment the driver of the team was also the sole operator of the equipment. When a formerly horse-drawn implement such as a mower was hitched to a tractor, however, it required one man to operate the mower and another to drive the tractor.

So, the previously self-sufficient farmer was compelled to hire a second man, or perhaps use a son, daughter, or wife to help with his field work.

During the late 1910s and early 1920s, companies manufactured and marketed ingenious arrangements of pulleys, ropes, and lines to solve these common problems.

However complex they appeared, they enabled the farmer to operate his tractor from the implement seat with some semblance of efficiency, making it a one-man operation again.

Of course, some implements—early reapers and gang plows—still made a two-man team almost a necessity.

From the turn of the century through the 1930s, the market experienced a proliferation of newly designed steam traction machines, gas tractors, and implements for farmers. Some implements were as small and simple as a motorized walking plow. At the other extreme was the 50-bottom Oliver plow pulled by a three-tractor hitch of OilPulls.

Producing tractors and related farm implements became a popular manufacturing practice. Every kind of company from automobile plants to washing machine factories jumped on the bandwagon. Many companies sold only one or two machines before they decided to abandon the cause and leave the market.

Economics, of course, played a major role in the extensive culling out of manufacturers. But the main reason was this was a time of experimentation, of discovery. Of the myriad designs presented, most unfortunately didn't work or didn't do the intended job.

Agriculture was changing, with more emphasis being placed on specialization. For example, large row-crop operations required different tractors and implements than extensive wheat farming operations. And many small farms had to have tractors and implements that combined small size, affordability, and efficiency.

Inventor-businessman Harry Ferguson wasn't the first person to envision farming implements as an integral part of the farm tractor. (This, incidentally, was an important milestone, perhaps second only to the concept of mechanical power itself.) But he was the only designer-manufacturer who persisted in this dream for 20 years until his three-point mounted hydraulic system and related equipment became a reality.

Harry Ferguson filed for a patent on his unique method of draft control in 1925. He then continued for more than two additional decades as an innovator and manufacturer of three-point mounted equipment, which has now become the standard for almost every tractor and implement manufacturer in the world.

The system is at work on tractors of all sizes, from the economy-sized to the supercharged tractor mounting eight giant tires and running a multi-cylinder diesel capable of more than 350 gross horsepower. The implements are also bigger and better designed for more effective usage as farming needs continually change.

The three-point mounted hydraulic system originally conceived by Irishman Henry Ferguson has stood the test of time to make it truly "the better way" for the world's farmers.

Progress on the search for a "better way" had evolved to this phase of animal power circa 3500 B.C. It left a lot to be desired and a long way to go before the three-point system emerged.

the Overtime tractor, an American-manufactured Waterloo Boy.

To boost sales, Ferguson and one of his employees, Willie Sands, began promoting the tractor by extensively demonstrating the machines throughout farming communities. They used their new tractor and whatever plows were available. As a result, the men were soon considered experts on farming equipment, especially plows.

Wartime Speeds Implement Development

In 1916–1917, all of Great Britain was facing a food shortage because of World War I. Many women were being pressed into farm work due to the shift of manpower for the armed forces. Also critical was the shift of horsepower, because draft horses were also vital to the war effort.

Ferguson's implement systems odyssey began in earnest in March 1917, when the Irish Board of Agriculture asked him to improve the efficiency of Ireland's tractors. What an opportunity!

In their new role, Ferguson and Sands gave plowing demonstrations throughout Ireland. Their objective was to help improve the efficiency of farming with tractors, and they were to evaluate the available tractors and equipment on a 10-point basis:

1. Weight of the machine.
2. Mechanical design and construction.
3. Quality of the plowing.
4. Time taken and the number of workers required.
5. Adaptability for plowing different widths and depths.
6. Adaptability to different kinds of work such as cultivating, harvesting, and road haulage.
7. Ease and simplicity of handling.
8. Ease of turning, and space and time required, and uniformity of furrow ends.
9. Facility and efficiency of attachment of tractor.
10. Price.

At the time, tractor design had evolved along the lines of its immediate predecessor, the steam traction engine, so tractors were large, heavy, and unwieldy machines generally ill-suited to solving the country's food production crisis.

Agricultural Implements Through the Ages

1701: Englishman Jethro Tull invents a mechanical seed planter.

1720: A patent is granted to Englishman Joseph Foljambe for an iron-sheathed moldboard.

1769: French inventor Nicholas Cugnot builds a self-propelled steam engine.

1797: Charles Newbold is issued a U.S. patent for a solid cast-iron plow.

1799: Englishman Joseph Boyce records an English patent for a mechanical reaper.

1819: The U.S. government issues a patent to Jethro Wood for a cast-iron plow he based on an earlier design of agriculturist and President Thomas Jefferson.

1833: Obed Hussey gets the first U.S. patent for a mechanical reaper.

1834: Cyrus H. McCormick is granted another U.S. patent for his mechanical reaper.

1837: John Lane makes plows using saw-blade steel.

1837: John Deere begins producing plows using saw-blade steel. With a partner he starts manufacturing the Grand Detour plow.

1846: John Deere sells his interest in the Grand Detour plow, then immediately starts Deere & Company in Moline, Illinois.

1850: McCormick purchases Hussey's reaper cutting bar patent.

1868: James Oliver designs a process for molding iron and then chilling it to produce a plow and mold board that scours cleaner.

1873: First U.S. self-propelled traction steam engine goes on sale by Battle Creek, Michigan, firm of Merritt and Kellogg.

1907: Ford Motor Company produces experimental "Automobile Plow."

1911: Introduction of the Hackney Auto Plow.

1912: John Deere develops an experimental motor plow.

1915: B. F. Avery debuts its Louisville Motor Plow.

1917: Harry Ferguson patents semimounted plow for Ford Eros conversion.

1925: Harry Ferguson files for patent on his unique method of draft control.

1928: John Deere introduces GP model with industry's first power lift for equipment such as planters and cultivators.

1936: Ferguson-Brown tractor is first to be manufactured with integral hydraulic system for three-point implements.

1939: Ford-Ferguson 9N tractor introduces hydraulic three-point system. Four implements are initially available: Seven-tine general-purpose cultivator, 10-inch 2-bottom plow, three-row ridger, and nine-tine row-crop cultivator.

1940 to 1960: Ford-Ferguson, Ferguson, Dearborn, and numerous aftermarket manufacturers design and produce an increasing number of varied implements and attachments for the three-point system. Eventually hundreds of all kinds and variations are available.

Tractors were viewed strictly as a replacement for horses. The only difference was that a towed implement was hitched to a drawbar instead of a doubletree. In many cases, the same implements had been hitched behind a team of horses just days or weeks earlier.

Ferguson initially believed that the era's large and heavy tractor was the largest obstacle to efficient plowing. After a while, though, he realized the big bottleneck was the plow itself.

There was no time to waste, because the German U-boats were drawing a tighter noose around the British Isles. They were sending shipload after shipload of food and other critical supplies to the bottom of the ocean.

While returning to Belfast with Sands, their Irish tour of tractors completed, Ferguson was immersed in thought. Then inspiration struck.

"There must be a better way of doing the job," he suddenly said to Sands. "We'll design a plough [plow]."

There's an interesting and revealing Ferguson quote and comment that begins Chapter Six of Colin Fraser's *Tractor Pioneer: The life of Harry Ferguson*:

"It is no more possible to design a plow which would be suitable for use with various sizes of tractors than it is to design a cart which can be drawn by donkey or a Clydesdale, or a body that would be suitable for all makes of cars."

The simple truth inherent in those words represented a novel idea when Ferguson laid them down as a guiding principle. Until then, plows had been built for use behind any tractor of any shape or any size. And, he culled another simple truth when he decided that a plow should become a unit with the tractor when it was hitched on: It should not be trailed along on a chain, like an afterthought.

To be able to recognize such truths that others have missed, and exploit them, is one of the hallmarks of genius. And, it is strange how, in retrospect, many of these truths seem so obvious that one is surprised they were not thought of earlier.

The business end of Harry Ferguson's concept. This type of hitch, in one form or another, graces nearly every farm tractor made in the entire world.

As early as 1912, Deere & Company, Moline, Illinois, was experimenting with a "motor plow," which certainly would meet the requirement of the unit principle. Then Deere & Company purchased the Waterloo Gasoline Engine Company in 1918. A possible link to Ferguson is that the Waterloo Gasoline Engine Company manufactured the Waterloo Boy tractor, called the Overtime in England, for which Ferguson was a dealer. The Hackney Auto Plow, which first appeared on the market in 1911, was another early tractor plow. Plows mounted underneath the tractor, such as the Birrell Motor Plow, were in production as early as 1910.

Was Ferguson aware of these designs? Nobody knows, and it doesn't really alter the big picture, because only Ferguson's design endured.

To begin his experiments on a better plow design and more maneuverable tractor, he chose the Eros tractor, a Model T Ford that could be converted to a tractor using a kit made by a St. Paul, Minnesota, firm. The Eros was obviously in the featherweight class compared to other available tractors.

A Radically Different Design

Ferguson's plow was a radical departure from plow designs of the time, as it weighed a third of its contemporaries' weights, was mounted directly to the Ford Eros tractor, and—wonder of wonders—it had no wheels. The entire plow could be raised and lowered, and plowing depth could be adjusted, from the tractor seat. And because the plow was hitched under the tractor, it helped keep the tractor wheels in better contact with the ground.

Ferguson called this close coupling of the tractor and implement the "unit principle." In November 1917, he gave the first public demonstration of his new plow design, the first recorded instance of a Ferguson mounted implement using the unit principle. It was built in the May Street premises of Harry Ferguson, Ltd.

The demonstration proved Ferguson's theory of the unit principle by plowing 5 to 6 inches deep at 2 1/2 miles per hour. This represented coverage of approximately four acres during a day's work. Meanwhile, a team of horses ahead of a single-bottom plow was hard-pressed to turn over even one acre in a day. To be sure, the system was still imperfect at this point, but the Ferguson unit principle demonstrably worked in real-world conditions, and over time it evolved into the perfected three-point system.

However, later that same year (1917) Ferguson's first plow immediately became outdated. A new tractor entered the United Kingdom market. A shipment of 6,000 Fordson tractors hit British soil, and Ferguson's implement system wasn't compatible with the tractor.

Not in the least discouraged, Harry sold what plows he could for Eros tractors. Meanwhile, he had Willie Sands design a way to convert the rest of the plows manufactured to mount on the Fordson tractor. The sale of these plows provided funds that allowed Ferguson and his team to work on a design specifically for the Fordson tractor.

This further evolution of his design resulted in the duplex hitch: two parallel bars, or struts, one above the other with the lower approximately in the position of a conventional drawbar.

This was a huge evolutionary step. It solved the problem of a tractor becoming "light in the front," because the top link of the hitching arrangement transferred pressure to the tractor. This, in effect, pushed the front end down. The heavier the draft on the plow, the more pressure that was applied to the front of the tractor.

However, the duplex system did not trail properly, so Sands, Archie Greer, and John Williams set to work with Ferguson designing further improvements.

They added a third link to help stabilize side drift. The first three-point mounting had two upper links with a single lower link that controlled the implement depth. The two upper links were used to raise and lower the implement. This arrangement helped stabilize the trailing problems.

Depth Control Remains a Challenge

Depth control was a continuing problem, one that Ferguson wanted to overcome without the use of a rear depth wheel on the plow. Success on this point seemed to defy his team's efforts, so they forged ahead, using the depth wheel until they could develop a better solution.

Their next step involved eliminating the balance spring and lever used to raise and lower the implement. Their aim was to have the tractor provide the source of power needed to lift the implement. When they filed a patent for this concept they included three designs: Electric, mechanical (using cone clutches), and a hydraulic system. The electric and mechanical methods soon proved impractical, so they concentrated their efforts on the hydraulic system.

With research and development work progressing nicely in Northern Ireland, Ferguson was making trips to the United States in search of a manufacturer who could mass-produce enough plows to meet the projected sales potential. In 1922, John Shunk, owner of a large blacksmith shop in Bucyrus, Ohio, agreed to put the Fordson plow into production. An agreement was signed amidst much banqueting and celebrating that was given press coverage in the local paper.

In a typical Harry Ferguson burst of optimism, he decided the sales target for the first year's production would be 50,000 units. Ferguson and his close friend, John Williams, then headed home to Northern Ireland, confident the plows would soon be rolling off the production line and sales would jingle dealership cash registers.

Probably before their ship docked, Shunk, possibly overwhelmed by Ferguson's production estimate, changed his mind. He wouldn't make 50,000 plows. In fact, he wouldn't make even *one* plow for Ferguson.

Ferguson set sail once again for the United States, this time approaching a manufacturer of disc, spring-tooth, and spike-tooth harrows. The company caught Ferguson's eye with its advertisements for implements built especially for the Fordson tractor.

Yes, the Roderick Lean Company of Mansfield, Ohio, was a natural to build Ferguson's plows, and an agreement was reached. Some of the parts for the plows were to be sublet to the Vulcan Plow Company, Evansville, Indiana.

Shortly after Ferguson returned home, another problem loomed. The first plows were outfitted with the troublesome depth wheel to regulate plowing depth. In certain conditions, the depth wheel interfered with the weight transfer to the tractor, causing the tractor to lose traction and allowing the wheels to spin. All concerned realized that wouldn't do at all.

The depth control problem that had plagued the design team from the beginning had to be solved, and quickly, too. Plows were being produced, and the plows already sold would have to be modified if the original buyers were to be retained as happy customers.

Willie Sands Finds a Solution

Sands had left the company in 1920 to open his own business, but two years as a businessman with all its attendant headaches was sufficient, and Sands was happy to resume working for Ferguson.

Sands' return was a boon for both men: Sands was doing what he did best, and Ferguson got his depth wheel problem solved, thanks to a brilliant floating skid that Sands designed. The skid was simple and inexpensive. It could be both retrofitted to existing plows and also easily adapted to plows during the manufacturing process.

The skid ran in the furrow bottom. It was linked to the tractor at the hitch point, which transferred the rise and fall of the rear tires to the plow depth.

This time Ferguson got at least a couple of years back home before a problem again gnawed at his plow production. In 1924, the Roderick Lean Company succumbed to financial difficulties and filed bankruptcy. However, the Roderick Lean Company published a sales brochure in 1925 which still listed the company as a supplier of Fordson implements. The company obviously was either refinanced or restructured, remaining in the implement manufacturing business. But, for whatever reason, the company discontinued producing plows for Ferguson. At this point, a lesser man might have given up. Not Ferguson.

Finding Yet Another Partner

In 1925 Ferguson returned to the United States, once again taking along his friend, John Williams. Their first visit was to the Sherman brothers, Eber and George. Ferguson wasn't a stranger to the Sherman brothers. They were the main Fordson tractor distributors for the state of New York, and they had met Ferguson previously.

They'd been following the news concerning Ferguson's plow design and they believed it was the solution. Predictably, Ferguson convinced them to enter into a partnership with him to manufacture and distribute plows. Ferguson-Sherman, Inc., was established in Evansville, Indiana, that same year, and production began in 1926. Finally, it seemed Ferguson had resolved his recurrent plow production troubles, but it was not to be. More dark clouds were gathering on his horizon, as noted in *The New Ferguson Album* by Colin E. Booth and Allan T. Condie:

Once plow production at Sherman Brothers in 1925 was running smoothly, Ferguson turned his attention to improving his system and adapting it so that various other implements other than plows could be used. The improvements were aimed at removing the balance spring and making the tractor do the work of lifting the implement. Various ideas were tried, including [an] electric

This display of Ferguson memorabilia includes an advertisement, farm sign, dealer signs, identification plate, and decals.

motor, and a mechanical system driven from the belt pulley through a couple of cone clutches, until finally a hydraulic system was devised.

This was fitted on the back of a Fordson tractor. Further work was done on the duplex linkage, which was first changed to a three-link system with single lower link and two upper links, with the lower link controlling the depth and the upper links lifting and lowering the implement, the linkage now being mounted on the tractor and not the implement.

Several companies were showing some interest in Ferguson's ideas including Allis Chalmers, Rushton, Ransome, and the Rover Car Company. The most fruitful talks took place with the Morris Motor Co., who agreed to build a tractor using the Ferguson hydraulic system, but at the last minute the agreement fell through.

The location of the hydraulic pump, however, did create one problem in that the hydraulics would only operate with the tractor in gear. One had to be on the move when raising the implements and this could be awkward at headlands when ploughing.

When Ford stopped U.S. production of the Fordson tractor in 1928, demand for, and thus production of, the plow also ceased. At this point Ferguson and his team had 10 trying, expensive years invested in the design of their revolutionary plow. On the plus side, they'd solved the tractor's traction problem by proving that a light tractor could derive needed traction from the plow design instead of tractor weight. Their design also prevented the tragedy of a tractor rearing up and over when the trailed plow hit an obstruction.

They had a workable depth control for the plow, too, although they were still unable to satisfactorily control working depth of the other ground-engaging implements they were designing. Ferguson was also convinced that the tractor, rather than the man, should do the work of lifting the implement.

The team still had a long way to go, especially considering that now both the only tractor to which their plow could be mounted was no longer being made. And, yet again, their source of the manufactured plow itself had dried up. But it just wasn't Ferguson's nature to let a couple of small details like that deter him from his dream of a better way for farmers. There was still time . . .

CHAPTER TWO

Success of the Three-Point System

A BREAKTHROUGH IN IMPLEMENT TECHNOLOGY

"The Ferguson System—Each attached implement becomes self-propelled and automatically controlled" sums up what Ferguson felt was the major advantage of his three-point concept. This is a Ferguson tractor, pull-type tandem disc, 11-shank rigid cultivator, 2-bottom plow, and 7-shank tiller.

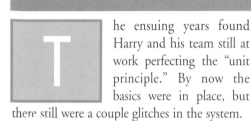

T he ensuing years found Harry and his team still at work perfecting the "unit principle." By now the basics were in place, but there still were a couple glitches in the system.

First of all, the system for raising and lowering the implement was not up to Ferguson's wishes. Even more critical was the continuing issue of the plow's depth control. Not being able to completely solve this problem was especially troubling because the other implements they were designing wouldn't work with their temporary solution of a skid to control working depth.

By this time, though, Ferguson and his team had focused on developing a hydraulic system to raise and lower implements. No tractor was available with the internal system they needed, so they developed their own—an external unit that could be bolted onto a Fordson tractor. Results may have been so-so at best, but they gave the team enough encouragement to continue the search.

Perhaps out of frustration, Ferguson and his team gave many plowing demonstrations with his plow fitted to a Fordson equipped with the external hydraulic system. While the results were mostly good, observers and potential customers seemed only to see the negative aspect. The upshot? Ferguson knew what he really needed was a tractor designed especially for his system.

Ferguson repeatedly tried—and failed—to interest manufacturers in building a tractor with an internal hydraulic system that would work

This "The Ferguson System" metal sign proudly hangs in the shop of a restorer.

exclusively with his hitching system and implements. Allis-Chalmers showed enough interest to execute an option, but then chose not to exercise that option. Other firms, such as the Rover Car Company and the Ransome Rapier Company, responded positively to Ferguson's pitches, yet there always seemed to be prevailing circumstances that prevented a deal being struck.

Ferguson and his two researchers, Willie Sands and Archie Greer, doggedly modified, tested, rejected, and yes, finally incorporated some design improvements in the draft control system. Anybody who knew Ferguson probably wasn't surprised by his next decision. If nobody was interested in building a tractor to his design, then he'd simply build his own tractor, one that would incorporate all his wants and desires. Work on the tractor began at the Harry Ferguson, Ltd., facilities on May Street in 1932.

Persistence Generates Working Capital

How was Ferguson able to finance his tractor and implement passion considering the many setbacks he'd endured over the previous 15 years? The only real "wealth" Ferguson possessed was the combination of his inventive abilities and his persuasive convictions about his work.

A little background: Back in 1911, when he and his brother parted ways, Ferguson's success with airplanes, motorcycles, and automobiles, caught the attention of moneyed and influential men, including McGregor Greer, John Williams, and others who provided capital for the new venture of Harry Ferguson, Ltd. The business prospered from the beginning. Ferguson ran a first-rate shop. Even those who were put off by his sometimes overbearing self-assurance respected his abilities. His attention to detail to satisfy the customer paid off in a steady flow of customers through the door.

After his first year in business, the company was incorporated, meaning it required a board of directors. This board was in constant conflict with Ferguson during the early years. It lacked Ferguson's enthusiasm for his tractor projects. The board saw these experiments as an ongoing cash drain, not revenue-producers.

Ferguson no doubt had controlling interest in the venture, though, because, despite the grumbling about lack of returns on the tractor projects, he forged onward, returns be damned.

The following letter from Eber Sherman to Henry Ford on March 2, 1939 provides insight into research, development and financing.

Proof of the soundness of the program [speaking of Harry Ferguson's vision of a new design of farming equipment] lies in the fact that we went to Evansville, Indiana, and formed a corporation known as Ferguson-Sherman, Inc. In spite of the advice of bankers and friends, we proceeded to manufacture and sell the "Unit Ferguson Plows" on S/D/B/L terms, which was heretofore unheard of in the implement industry.

Sales in 1926 were slightly less than one quarter of a million dollars [$250,000]. Sales in 1927 were more than four hundred thousand dollars [$400,000] according to Eber Sherman. In 1928, a program had been worked out with inventories providing for doubling 1927 sales.

Unfortunately, in January 1928, the tractor for which the plow was designed was withdrawn from the market almost overnight. This completely altered our expansion program. Ferguson-Sherman, Inc., was no longer able to advance the two percent of sales for research and experimentation for the major expansion which the design of our large-scale operation called for.

A letter from Eber Sherman stated that two percent of sales was earmarked for research and development of the Ferguson System. Sherman places sales for the two years at roughly $650,000. Research and development's two percent would be approximately $13,000. That would have bought a considerable amount of research back in 1928. Ferguson evidently thought so, too. When the Fordson was suddenly withdrawn from the market, shrinking the demand for Ferguson and Sherman implements, the Shermans wrote Ferguson asking to be relieved of their two percent obligation. Ferguson was initially not sympathetic to their situation, but later waived the royalty obligation.

Sands and Greer were the two members of the design team who found ways to incorporate Ferguson's design ideas and fix the problems that cropped up. This same philosophy

A varied array of Ferguson implements is displayed. They are, from left: one-way disc plow, feed mill, two-bottom plow, one-bottom plow, flip-flop two-way plow, orchard cultivator, lister with potato planter, large three-disc plow, and sprayer.

was bound to carry over to the money people—concerning income, expenses, and cash flow—when Ferguson had ideas or problems. He almost certainly figured it was their job to find a way to make it happen, and if problems arose, to find the fix.

A Manufacturing Agreement

It wasn't until actually much later that the board of Harry Ferguson, Ltd., decided there was indeed some potential for the tractor and implement projects. In the meantime, Ferguson worked out ventures with other companies, such as Ferguson-Sherman and Ferguson-Brown. This gave him more freedom to operate without going to the Harry Ferguson, Ltd., board.

In 1933, the first tractor with an internal hydraulic system linked to a three-point hitching system was finished. Painted all black, it became known as the "Black tractor." With the "Black tractor" and its plow, the hydraulically controlled three-point system was virtually complete. It was the combination that in the coming decades would be copied by nearly every tractor and implement manufacturer in the world. However, Ferguson and his team never considered themselves manufacturers, nor did they really have the desire to be manufacturers. Their forte was research and design, plus Ferguson's sales prowess.

So immediately after the Black tractor was finished, Ferguson set about finding someone to manufacture the tractor and implements. He succeeded in interesting and contracting with David Brown of Huddersfield, England, to manufacture the tractor and implements while Harry Ferguson, Ltd.—a business established in Huddersfield—would market them.

David Brown Tractors, Ltd. was a large company with a reputation for manufacturing gears of the highest quality. Ferguson had earlier contracted with Brown to manufacture gears for the Black tractor, and again, Fergu-

18

Ferguson System Patents

U nited Kingdom patents granted to Harry George Ferguson, Donegal Square East, Belfast, Northern Ireland, with application date, patent number, and feature patented:

September 12, 1917, 119883: Arrangement for direct hitching and controlling plow, including the first top link.

February 1, 1918, 122703: Improvements to above. Now known as the "Belfast" plow hitch. Transfers tractor weight to plow to ensure proper depth.

December 15, 1919, 160248: Two-point linkage or "Duplex" hitch by way of both upper and lower links set to converge to affect line of draft forward of rear axle, depth controlled by varying length of upper link. The first "virtual hitch point" system plus first partial overload release by weight transfer.

June 28, 1921, 186172: As 160248, but with depth wheel.

November 3, 1921, 195421: Modified 160248 allowing draft to balance penetration via spring mechanism.

December 11, 1923, 226033: The ultimate version of 160248 "Duplex" hitch employing automatic mechanical depth control via slipper in furrow bottom linked to linkage. Achieved full weight transfer while retaining safety features of 160248.

February 12, 1925, 253566: "Master patent" incorporates the principle of "draft" control whereby the depth of a ground-engaging implement is automatically controlled by reference to the effort or draft needed to pull it. Means of linkage movement to be effected by electric, mechanical or hydraulic device. Also covers draft control by means of tractor's transmission torque.

July 3, 1928, 320084: Converging three-point linkage plus front furrow width control via cranked cross-shaft. The second dimension to 160248.

July 3, 1933, 421983: Improved efficiency tractor transmission using internally toothed ring gear reduction (as used on Black and "A") plus power take-off (PTO) driven from final drive (ground-speed PTO) placed centrally over drawbar plate plus belt pulley drive plus internally mounted dual ram draft control using 253566.

February 5, 1936, 470069: Hydraulic draft control by placing the control valve on suction side of an oil-immersed pump to avoid aeration and heating of oil. Simple "flow on demand" system.

February 5, 1936, 471515: Check chains/antisway blocks for three-point linkage that allows lateral movement in work, but limits sway when raised.

February 5, 1937, 470087: Development of 253566 and 470069—incorporates automatic release of hydraulic pressure to protect implement on hitting obstruction.

November 30, 1937, 510352: Major transmission improvements by incorporating a constant running lay shaft in gearbox, thus allowing PTO and hydraulic pump to be driven whenever clutch is engaged whether in gear or not, plus pump driven before or after dog clutch plus engine drive PTO plus restatement of PTO shaft position as per 421983 rearwards within the three-point linkage.

These are by no means all the Harry Ferguson patents, but just the principle ones that relate to his three-point system. Many more of his patents related to specific implements. Interestingly enough, Henry Ford actually held a larger number of patents on the Ford-Ferguson tractor than did Ferguson. None, however, dealt with the three-point system.

(Ferguson patent list, and permission to use same, granted by Massey Ferguson Tractors, Ltd., Coventry, England.)

---

son's enthusiasm and persuasive powers had made him a winner.

As the tooling at David Brown's plant gathered momentum, Ferguson's "better way" of the unit principle and three-point implements was about to be offered to the world.

Today, 8- and 10-bottom three-point plows on 350-horsepower tractors working in fields with acreage measured in quarter sections, half sections, and multiple sections aren't an uncommon sight on farms in many parts of the world. Agriculture, like every other industry on earth, has changed with awesome speed. However, remember that as recently as 50 years ago,

teams of horses were still the motive power on many U.S. farms. That will help you fully appreciate the magnitude of Ferguson's three-point system and the implements that were introduced with the Ferguson-Brown tractor.

Any system or tool that can quadruple one person's productivity is revolutionary at any time, regardless of how primitive it may appear years later. Consider that as you consider the size and design of the implements that appeared with the introduction of the Ferguson-Brown Type A tractor in 1936. The debut of the system was carried out with Ferguson's customary fanfare. The aggressive sales

and demonstration program that was launched immediately also helped.

This tractor was painted gray and had four three-point implements that made up the Ferguson System of farming. Available was a 10-inch, 2-bottom plow; a 7-spring tine cultivator; a 9-tine rigid tine cultivator; and a 3-row ridger. Later 12-inch, 2-bottom and 16-inch, single-bottom plows were added to the line.

Several accessories were designed to make the tractor more versatile around the farm. They included 6-inch row crop wheels, spring-mounted road bands for steel wheels with lugs, a belt pulley and patented adjustable rear wheels with rubber tires, and an extension drawbar.

The top three-point link was shorter than the later Ferguson type. The implement's top linkage coupling point had a small shield behind the coupling. Also, the swivel balls were held in place by a separate plate riveted to the lower links. The design of these implements remained virtually unchanged when they were produced as the next generation of implements for the Ford-Ferguson tractor.

Producing the Ferguson

Before covering the Ford-Ferguson implements, this excerpt from an article titled "Producing the Ferguson Tractor" in the November 1, 1938, issue of *The Implement and Machinery Review* put the design and manufacturing excellence of the tractors and implements into context.

Most things in agricultural engineering are evolutionary. But Harry Ferguson's hydraulically-controlled three-point hitch arrangement was revolutionary. Today, almost every farm tractor in the world goes out the manufacturer's door with some version of a three-point hitch.

It is now something like two years since the "Ferguson" tractor was put on a serious production basis after the preliminary experimental machines, which had been tried out in different parts of the country, had established beyond question the efficiency of the extremely novel principle involved. So now it is opportune to inquire what steps have been taken in the meantime from the production standpoint to place the machine on the market and to ensure that it is adequately "serviced."

The launching of the 'Ferguson' tractor on the market thus started under favorable auspices. For it was a distinctive type of machine and its manufacturing progress was sponsored by a firm whose reputation was immediately accepted as a guarantee of quality. Naturally enough, the production policy was not meteoric; it was too painstaking and thoughtful to become that, and, moreover, nothing so superficial was ever intended. Careful planning prepared the way, and similar instructed control throughout has built well upon foundation so excellently planned.

Proof of this—and impressive proof, too—is contained in the bold statement that, this year to date, no fewer than 750 sets of

"Ferguson" machinery have been sold! Further, there is more in this than meets the eye at first glance, for in selling "Ferguson" it is not only a tractor that is involved but, as our readers are so well aware, a new system of power-farming, in which specially designed implements, such as plow, cultivator, ridger, and so forth, are all concerned.

Achievement there is indeed in salesmanship that has succeeded in so relatively short a time in placing such a large number of complete sets in the hands of farmers, and upon it we offer our sincere congratulations to the general manager of the company, Mr. Walter L. Hill, who has handled the marketing of the equipment in all its stages from production to the most minute service detail, with a thoroughness and competence that have not only earned this success, but have also betrayed a most intimate knowledge of the tractor industry and power-farming.

As we have suggested, there is an impressive solidity and confidence about the production of the "Ferguson." A visit to the

works immediately conveys this atmosphere, for the "Ferguson-Brown" concern, although an obvious offshoot of Messrs. Its works have a floor space covering no less than an acre, all exclusively devoted to the production of the "Ferguson" power-farming equipment.

Materials are drawn from outside, as in the case of those in which the associated firm excel, but the tractor and allied equipment are all made in the "Ferguson-Brown" works, where the organization is a triumph for scientific and enlightened management. Few works in this country are so excellently arranged, so compact, and so modern, since here manufacturing had to be planned right from the most primary stages, which, while demanding much thought and detail, also had the advantage of permitting nothing but the most modern plant and layout to be employed.

Enormous sums have been spent on machinery of the latest description. The spacious and well-arranged machine shop is eloquent proof of this. Here are some wonderful

A beautiful ad concept is displayed in this ad with photograph enhanced by simple line drawings: "The Ferguson System turned the tractor into a farming machine."

tools! No less than £7,000 were expended on one machine alone, a "Bullard Mult-au-matic," which is for repetition jobs, and which we saw operating in multiple fashion on the cluster gears.

A blank enters at one stage and ends up after a series of progressive operations as the finished article entirely untouched by hand, and with the procedure uninterrupted as successive blanks enter and pass through the different stages continuously.

. . . Next we passed to the implement assembly floor, where the special plows, cultivators, row-crop tools, and other essential details are prepared for dispatch. Two coats of paint are used in the paint section, the undercoat being of a distinctive brown color to ensure that the grey finishing coat is completely applied, thereby ensuring definite protection against rust. The painting, too, is executed as to impart what used to be accepted in the implement trade as "show finish."

Before production of the Ferguson-Brown tractor and implements were discontinued in 1938, approximately 1,250 tractors and 5,000 implements were manufactured and sold. There are three reasons for the demise of the Ferguson-Brown tractor. It was costly, compared to other tractors available; it had some significant flaws (The tractor had to be moving for the hydraulics to the implement to operate. Thus, the tractor had to be in motion to lift the implement up and down. This made the implement difficult to manipulate in many situations.); and Ferguson and Brown's management experienced some differences of opinion that proved too strong to overcome.

Right top: A Ferguson tractor and three-point plow demonstration show that the development process of the Ferguson System is just about complete.

Right: A well-dressed Ferguson demonstrates that with rear-mounted three-point equipment, a field can be plowed completely, well into the corners. *Ford Motor Company Photomedia*

CHAPTER THREE

George and Eber Sherman

THE CONDUIT BETWEEN HENRY FORD & HARRY FERGUSON

Roderick Lean Manufacturing Company, Mansfield, Ohio, produced this non three-point hitch 14-inch, 2-bottom, duplex-hitch plow for Ferguson-Sherman Manufacturing Corporation. It was a manual-lift plow that was marketed just before the switch to three-point equipment. It was later adapted to the external hydraulics on the Fordson tractor's PTO. It is the only such plow known to still exist.

erguson's three-point concept faced all the same hurdles that confront many radically new products. The idea was as yet unproved in the minds of the farmers, who descended from uncountable generations relying on horses to farm. And at the time, farming wasn't an especially profitable venture, especially on the small farms for which the Ferguson-Brown tractor was designed.

Even more difficult to overcome was the need for farmers to purchase new implements to fit the tractor if they were to take full advantage of the Ferguson system. This extra expense was a decided obstacle to successful marketing, because by this time the Fordson tractor was again being produced at a new factory in Dagenham, Essex, England. The Fordson cost £135 on steel wheels or £180 on rubber tires. This was substantially less than the introductory price of £224 for the Ferguson-Brown, plus the implements added £26 each.

By 1938, David Brown and Ferguson called it quits. Brown decided to build his own tractor, incorporating some features that he'd proposed for the Ferguson-Brown tractor. Ferguson opposed the changes even though they proved to offer decided improvements. This disagreement may not have been the only cause for discontinuing the relationship, but it surely was part of it. The David Brown tractor was manufactured

The mark of distinction is the name of Ferguson on an implement identification plate. This duplex plow was manufactured by Roderick Lean Manufacturing Company for Ferguson.

with three-point linkage, but it couldn't be equipped with the hydraulic draft control that was covered by Ferguson's patent.

Even though production of the Ferguson-Brown ceased, the world now had the three-point system on its doorstep. But it would still be a couple of years before farmers could fully appreciate the new technology.

Fortunately, there were those who recognized what they were seeing. Even more fortunate, three of those people were in a position to do something about it. One, of course, was Henry Ford, and the other two were the Sherman brothers, Eber and George. Although less well known, they still played major roles in forging the partnership between Ford and Ferguson. From this partnership sprang the famous Ford-Ferguson tractor and its accompanying implement line.

The Sherman Brothers' Invaluable Contacts

How major a role did the Sherman brothers play? If not for them, Ferguson may not have had the opportunity for such a timely audience with Ford. The famous handshake and resulting partnership might never have happened.

Someone once said that timing is everything. For Ferguson, 1937 and 1938 was everything.

In 1937, Ford was 74 years old, yet was once again pursuing his youthful dream of tractor design and production, proclaiming: "What the country needs right now is a good tractor that will sell for around $250." Ford didn't have such a tractor. And his design team didn't appear to be close to Ford's dream tractor, even though he held a press conference in January to announce a new three-wheel design with a V-8 engine. This design was soon set aside and work began on another tractor, and then another.

Ford was ready to build a tractor—if only he could develop the right one.

Fate dealt Ford a harsh blow, and his health began to deteriorate. In 1938, he suffered his first stroke. Also, the clouds of war were looming on the horizon. Europe underwent restrictions on manufacturing supplies. Ford's second stroke, in 1941, left open only a small window of time.

Had the Ferguson-Ford meeting occurred any earlier than 1938, Ford might not have been open to, and ready for, tractor production; much

The power brokers discuss the Ferguson tractor after the famous "handshake agreement" at Fair Lane. George Sherman is standing behind the tractor next to the man wearing a hat. Harry Ferguson's back is facing the camera; to Ferguson's right is Charles Sorenson and Eber Sherman.
Ford Motor Company Photomedia

later, and his second stroke would have prevented him from re-entering the tractor business.

Along with timing, it doesn't hurt to have contacts in the right places. Ferguson knew the Shermans, and they knew Ford.

Some excerpts from the letters exchanged between Ferguson, in Ireland, and the Sherman brothers in the U.S. during 1929 bring into focus part of the relationship between the three parties and how much Ferguson relied on and

trusted the Shermans to deal with Ford. One letter also demonstrates just how long Ferguson and the Shermans had been courting an anticipated Ferguson-Ford relationship. It was written 10 years before the handshake agreement. The device being discussed is the externally mounted hydraulic system for the Fordson tractor and the duplex plow.

Here are some excerpts from Ferguson's letter to Eber Sherman:

1. If we attempt to wait on Ford's approval for our new device, he will merely take that as weakness on our part, and keep postponing and fooling us along. Therefore, it would seem we should go ahead, and market our complete device ourselves on the Fordson tractor.

   I agree that Ford is our easiest outlet now, and that you must play with them to some extent. If, however, you play too deeply with them and oversell Mr. Ford on our new invention he will most likely quit altogether.

2. One of the worst dangers is asking us to confine to the Ford Company. This will be continually suggested, and if we work ourselves into a position where we have to give a definite "no," then we may be in trouble. Smith actually started to ask me to confine to Ford, and then changed his mind, and said he would not raise the point until he came to Ireland.

   I am covering this point this morning because it is essential we should all give the same answer. That answer should be to point out that the extent to which the Ford Company will get a monopoly depends on themselves. If they make the right tractor, in the right volume, and give the right cooperation, then it would certainly be all to our interests to work together, but as they could not give any guarantees to do this thing and as they might change their policy or Mr. Ford might die or quit making tractors, obviously we could not commit ourselves, but we are with them 100 percent.

   A little courtesy and tact on this issue will do a lot if Mr. Ford is not firmly and absolutely convinced that we have solved the power farming problem 100 percent, and are his masters.

3. Put yourself in Mr. Ford's position. Would you commit yourself to manufacture millions of tractors, where another fellow could raise his finger and stop you any time he liked? I know I could not, and reckon I am a more trusting and less suspicious character than friend Henry; all of which goes to indicate how warily you must step.

4. The right course to follow is just to keep them sufficiently tickled with our work to get their cooperation until we have made our name and then we are safe.

5. Nothing, therefore, could exceed the wisdom of having connections other than Ford on which we can fall back, and I hope and believe that you and George have the good sense to see this.

6. If there were another small tractor with which we could cooperate, I think we should do it, but at this time that might seriously handicap your work.

7. I was just thinking a few days ago that if there were some new type of tractor with which we could cooperate and which would not bother the Ford crowd, we ought to do it. Then came George's letter about the little crawler. It would seem to me that we might soon cooperate with those people, and let them have our power device. As their type of tractor is outside anything Ford will ever do, he cannot well grouse, and as we might make a very useful friend there in case of trouble, let us consider this.

Then, the Shermans corresponded with Ford on March 2, 1939.

Dear Mr. Ford:

Attached are brief histories of George and I you requested over the phone.

I am sorry these couldn't have been sent sooner, but as explained, I left for Salt Lake City last Friday and just returned.

The Distributors that met me there are more than encouraged over prospects of the future after hearing the message I brought them of activities here.

You can be assured we here are doing all possible to complete the redesigning work on the new tractor and implements, so to have something to show you on your return.

The Brothers' Biographies

Eber Sherman enclosed two biographies (excerpted here) with his letter to Henry Ford, Eber's own, followed by that of his brother George.

On March 2, 1939, Eber Sherman wrote that he was "born July 26, 1888, at Willis, Michigan.

My early life was spent in companionship with my brother, George, who is only a year and a half younger than I am . . .

When it came time for us to branch out on careers of our own, I followed a sales career in the automotive industry, whereas George went into production and general business in an entirely different field.

In July, 1909, I was employed as order clerk for the Ford Motor Company, which at that time had its headquarters at the Piquette Avenue Plant . . .

In the summer of 1913 [I was sent] to New York, where I took over the management of the foreign department at 18 Broadway, and remained there until the spring of 1918.

I then left the employ of the Ford Motor Company at Mr. Ford's request to handle the details incident to the shipment of the first 6,000 Fordson tractors, which had been sold to the British Government to help win the war.

The shipment of these tractors was completed in July, 1918, and it was then at Mr. Ford's suggestion that I became actively identified with the sale of tractors and tractor implements as a distributor. I accepted the distributorship of the Fordson tractor for the whole of South America and the West Indies, and proceeded to organize the territory . . .

Our South American activities not only included the distribution of the Fordson tractor in Latin America, but we also held a distributor's concession for Ford Motor Company products for the entire State of Rio Grande do Sul, Brazil. We organized a company for this branch of the business known as 'Companhia Sulford,' with headquarters at Port Alegre.

We had a small assembly plant there and appointed our dealers through six

Although the Ford, Dearborn, and Ferguson plows share much of the same heritage, there are a number of die hard Ferguson fans that collect only Ferguson implements and memorabilia, such as this clock.

wholesale branches strategically located throughout the territory. Sales were built up from around 50 units to over 3,000 units per year, up to the time of the discontinuance of the company in 1926. During the 2 1/2 years that Sherman and Sheppard held the Fordson tractor concession in South America, they pioneered and sold throughout the territory over 3,000 Fordsons.

When the Ford Motor Company branches in 1921 took over the distribution of the Fordson throughout the world, I then branched out as an exporter of agricultural and special equipment for Fordson tractors, first concentrating on Europe and South America, and later extending activities throughout

the world. At one time our foreign sales were running well over $1 million per year.

It was during the time that my interests were solely in the export business that I became acquainted with Mr. Harry G. Ferguson and his New Principle of Farm Mechanization.

I was so impressed with his sincerity and his faith in what could be done, that I sought out my brother George, and together we made an independent survey of Mr. Ferguson's Principle, which resulted in our joining up with him and the formation of Ferguson-Sherman, Inc., of Evansville, Indiana, which was organized to manufacture and distribute

throughout the world the Ferguson unit hand-operated plow.

We did not go into the plow business at that time, but envisioned a new industry destined to be the largest in the world. Our program was a world program and was economically sound because:

1. It dealt with the largest and most basic industry in the world—agriculture.
2. Mr. Ferguson had discovered and formulated a principle in the field of mechanized farming that was diametrically opposed to the horse-drawn principle . . .
3. The Ferguson principle applied to farm tractors and unit implements was destined to mechanize the farms of the world because it could outperform the horse, both from an economical and practical standpoint.
4. A farm tractor was in production in sufficient volume at the time so that the one implement—a hand-operated plow, which was a compromise of the basic idea—could be sold at a profit sufficient to carry on the research experimental work, and inventions necessary for a complete world program of farm mechanization.

Unfortunately, in January 1928, the tractor for which the plow was designed was withdrawn from the market almost overnight. This completely altered our expansion program. Ferguson-Sherman, Inc., was no longer able to advance the two percent of sales for research and experimentation for the major expansion which the design of our large-scale operation called for.

When production of the Fordson tractor was discontinued in this country in 1928, Sherman and Sheppard supplied the gap between the discontinuance of production here and the time when production was started again in Cork by purchasing surplus stocks of tractors from dealers in this country and shipping them abroad. The exporting of these tractors also acted as a substitute for the loss in sales of agricultural and industrial tractor equipment.

Production of the Fordson tractor, which had been transferred from Dearborn to Cork, began in late 1929, and as the new policy of distribution in this country was to sell the tractors through independent distributors, I was selected to handle the distribution in New England and New York State.

This appointment was very timely, as due to the world economical collapse in 1929 and the tightening of money, it became increasingly difficult to maintain our export terms of draft against documents. We steadfastly refused to give terms, and as progress was made in developing our Fordson distributorship concession, we gradually withdrew from the export business, so that today Sherman and Sheppard handles no export business whatsoever.

In January 1934, I was called to Detroit and offered the national distributorship of the Fordson tractor for the entire United States. This offer I accepted, as I saw here the opportunity for laying the groundwork of building an organization of distributors and dealers to handle the new development of farm mechanization, which had been our vision since 1925, and which I knew in time Mr. Ferguson would eventually work out.

I proceeded along this line, as I knew that the best interests of the world at large rested in Mr. Ford and Mr. Ferguson joining hands together in the one major industry yet to come.

Finally Mr. Ferguson solved all the problems of outperforming the horse with a new lightweight tractor and hydraulically governed implements, and formed an English company in 1936 and started to manufacture and distribute in Great Britain the Ferguson Tractor and Hydraulically Controlled Unit Implements envisioned by us in 1925.

When a sufficient time had elapsed for these tractors and implements to prove themselves in actual operation in the hands of farmers under a wide variety of conditions, George went to England and made an exhaustive survey of the developments there. His findings are fully covered in the confidential report made to me.

I am so firmly convinced that the new Ferguson Hydraulic Principle is the answer to the farmers' problems that I believe that history will record the year 1939 as the date of the beginning of a new epoch for agriculture and the betterment of the world as a whole.

George Sherman also wrote in March 1939, "I was born on February 7, 1890, at Hand Station, a few miles southwest of Dearborn, Michigan." After gaining managerial and manufacturing experience with Kemi-Weld Can Company in Detroit; American Can Company in Joliet, Illinois; and Demountab Typewriter Company, Eber met his brother in Detroit in 1925 for a unique and new business opportunity.

In early 1925 my brother, Eber, asked me to meet him in Detroit, where he proceeded to tell me of the opportunity that we had to do something for the farmer, through the Ferguson principle. It was then that we made a survey and decided to join Mr. Harry G. Ferguson, of Belfast, Ireland, on a journey of mechanizing the farms of the world.

In December 1925, I went to Evansville, Indiana, and negotiated a Cost Plus Contract with the Vulcan Plow Company, of Evansville, which had all the elements of a lasting association with them, but being accustomed to well-organized methods of manufacturing parts to established tolerances, I could not countenance the standards prevailing in the implement industry, so that due to their failure to manufacture the parts for us to standards that we laid down, we were forced eventually to take over most of the manufacture ourselves.

Manufacturing processes were improved all down the line, with a consequent reduction in cost, and the future looked bright until the discontinuance of the production of the Fordson in this country, which meant complete loss of volume.

I do not know how we have managed to keep Ferguson-Sherman, Inc., alive all these years, but we carried on somehow, as we were determined to keep the Ferguson principle, as expressed in the hand-operated plow, before the farmer buying public until the new tractor and hydraulically operated implements could prove themselves in England.

Mr. Ferguson had kept both my brother and me informed of the progress being made on the other side, and I finally went to England in August 1937, skeptical of the reports that I had been receiving.

I took no one's word for anything, but made an independent survey, keeping uppermost in my mind that we must now prove that the Ferguson principle is capable of displacing the horse, which meant that we must outperform the horse, wherever the horse can work, from both a practical and economical standpoint. The result of this survey is expressed in the report to my brother dated October 17, 1937.

CHAPTER FOUR

Ferguson and Ford form an Alliance

THE THREE-POINT SYSTEM UNDER FORD'S MICROSCOPE

"Certainly I can operate it!" is what the young girl seems to be saying to Henry Ford as he inspects a 9N tractor with attached Ferguson System three-point implement. *Ford Motor Company Photomedia*

By now the story of the famous handshake agreement is part of every Ford-Ferguson collector's repertoire. Ferguson demonstrated a tractor and plow design that worked. Ford saw a system that worked.

Both men were highly intuitive in their design endeavors. So it was no great leap of faith for Ford to buy what he saw that day in 1938 at Fair Lane, Michigan. Ferguson just "knew" it was a revolutionary design, and Ford just "knew" it would work.

However, not everyone at the Ford Motor Company "knew" it would work or was as convinced as Ford. Someone, and probably not Ford, ordered an engineering study on the Ferguson system to determine if it would work, and just how it would work. It was the first time Harry Ferguson's system had been reduced to definable lab results. In his "Report on Ferguson Plow Linkage," Albert O. Roberts wrote:

The Ferguson method of attaching an implement to the rear end of a tractor employs parallel links instead of the conventional pivoted beams. The purpose of this study is to investigate what influence this has on weight transfer, traction, minimum tractor weight, and safety for the operator.

When plowing 6 inches deep, the links stand in the position shown in Fig. 1. The forces set up in the links in this position have an

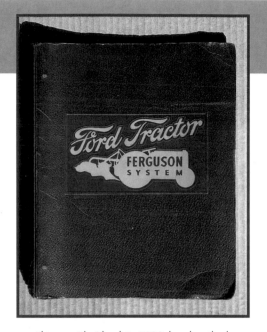

This was "the" book in 1939 that described in detail the Ford 9N tractor and the available Ferguson System implements.

upward component of 86 pounds per 1,000 pound draft. This force decreases as the plow goes deeper. When plowing about 9 inches deep, the lower link becomes horizontal.

Therefore, the vertical component of the stress in this link is 0, but the upper link still has an upward component of 80 pounds per 1,000 pound draft.

This upward component of the forces in the linkage is always far less than the weight of the plow (308 pounds for the 14-inch two-bottom). Also, there is a downward force of about 200 pounds (estimated) per 1,000 pound draft due to the weight of the soil lifted and the force necessary to break

the soil out and cut the furrow slice. This force is sometimes called the suction of the plow; 308 pounds [plus] 200 pounds [minus] 86 pounds [equals] 422 pounds.

Unless the soil is hard enough to offer 400 pounds resistance to the weight and suction of the plow, we always have a force holding the plow to the maximum depth allowed by the adjustable limiting device on the tractor frame. This device is a hydraulic ram, which automatically compensates for uneven ground by maintaining a constant draft. In uniform, level soil, the ram remains fixed, so in the model we have used a set screw to represent it.

Transfer of Weight

Since the linkage is normally fixed as shown above, in analyzing for transfer of weight from one axle to the other, we may assume the plow is rigidly fixed to the tractor frame. This is the unique advantage in the Ferguson linkage. The plow functions as if it were rigidly fixed to the tractor frame instead of being pivoted to it and still it moves up and down to suit the tilting or pitching of the tractor on uneven ground.

In Figure 2, a study is made of a 1/4-size model suspended in air by [six] external forces: 1. gravity, 2. front axle support, 3. rear axle support, 4. traction of rear wheels, 5. draft of plow, [and] 6. suction of plow.

Henry Ford, left, and Harry Ferguson, right, discuss the merits of the Ferguson System while a model used to demonstrate the draft control principle sits on the table between them. When Ford saw the Ferguson demonstration at Fair Lane in 1938, he asked that the table be brought from the house. It was at this table that the famous "handshake agreement" took place.

The spring interposed between the rear wheels and the frame represents the driving torque. The horizontal line of draft will be approximately on the line of traction when one wheel is in the furrow, as explained in Fig. 3. In this experiment, the rolling resistance is disregarded so that the entire torque is used to produce draft on the plow.

The horizontal draft and the vertical plow suction are considered separately, for there is motion and work being done along the horizontal line, but the vertical force is static. The resultant of these two forces is sometimes called the "Draft of the Plow," but in this discussion when we speak of plow draft we mean the force which moves the plow, and this force is horizontal.

It is interesting to note that under these conditions the axle torque has no lifting effect on the front end. As shown in the table, there was no transfer of weight though the torque was changed from 0 to 68 pounds.

That portion of the axle torque which is used to pull the plow has no lifting effect on the front end. This is obvious from Fig. 2, and still it seems odd to be able to screw the nut on the torque spring down without forcing the front end of the tractor up. The reaction of the torque on the frame (i.e., that part of the torque which is converted into draft) is entirely balanced out by the plow linkage.

The linkage gives the same effect as if the plow and tractor frame were all one piece, as shown in Fig. 2. This figure is drawn this way to make the facts more obvious, although in the experiment, 1/4-size links are used, as in Fig. 1, and all pivots were fitted with anti-friction needle bearings.

If the horizontal plow draft is below the rolling plane of the tractor wheels, there will be a transfer of weight from the rear wheels to the front.

So far, we have discussed only the effect of that part of the torque which is pulling the plow. The power which goes to overcome friction in motor, transmission, rear axle, and rear wheel bearings has no effect on weight transfer, but the friction in the front wheels and the rolling resistance of the four wheels in the field are overcome by rear axle torque, and this torque transfers a small amount of weight from the front to the rear.

It takes 457 pounds to tow the Fordson tractor across the field with the plow raised out of the ground. If we make deduction for the rear axle friction which should not be included, the lighter Ferguson tractor (2,184 pounds with plow) would probably have a rolling resistance of about 300 pounds. The 38-inch rear wheels have a rolling radius of about 19 inches when the lugs are buried in the soil, so the rear axle torque necessary to overcome the rolling resistance will be 19 [times] 300 pounds [equals] 5,700 pound inches.

Since the wheelbase is 69 inches, the lifting effect on the front axle will be 5,700/69 (5,700 over 69) [equals] 82 1/2 pounds. In other words, about 82 pounds are transferred from the front to the rear axle by the torque which drives the tractor when the plow is suspended above the ground.

The total weight of the tractor and plow is 2,134 pounds, and the center of gravity of the whole unit is only 20.3 inches ahead of the rear axle. This means that 70 percent of the total weight is on the rear axle before the torque is applied.

The plow not only adds its own 308 pounds to the rear axle but balances off 168 pounds from the front to the rear. 308 [times] 37.5 /69 [equals] 168 pounds.

Weight on front with plow—644 [pounds]

Weight on rear with plow—1,540 [pounds]

Weight on front without plow—812 [pounds]

Weight on rear without plow—1,064 [pounds]

There is an advantage here over the wheel-type plow. Instead of carrying the plow on wheels of its own, this weight is carried on the rear tractor wheels, giving additional traction and making it possible to use a lighter tractor.

As mentioned above, there is another force called plow suction, which also transfers weight from the front to the rear. This will vary with the weight and condition of the soil, but will be about 20 percent of the horizontal force which moves the plow. The horizontal force is the only one which is doing work, for the motion of the plow is in a horizontal direction.

"Therefore, the plow suction, [times] vertical force, may be considered simply an added weight on the plow. For 1,000 pounds draft, the suction would be about 200 pounds. This 200 pounds would transfer 200 [times] 37.6 / 69 [equals] 109 pounds from the front to the rear axle.

Summing up all the forces which affect weight distribution, we have (see table below):

1,000 pounds draft

	Front	Rear
Original weight without plow	812	1,064
Added weight of plow	+308	
Transferred by weight of plow	-168	+168
Transferred by pull of plow	0	0
Transferred by rolling resistance	-82	+82
Added plow suction	0	+200
Transferred by plow suction	-109	+109
Total [pounds]	453	1,931

It can be readily seen from the above table and from Fig. 2 that the tractor can never be turned over backward by increased plow draft should the plow strike a stump. In fact, since the line of draft will usually be below the rolling plane of the tractor wheels, the plow helps hold the front end down.

All the above considerations apply to the operation of the tractor on fairly level fields. When steep grades are encountered, more weight will be transferred from the front to the rear for now a large percentage of the axle torque is used to lift the tractor, the implement, and the operator. If the total weight is 2,350 pounds and the grade 30 percent or 16.7 degrees, the drawbar pull necessary to do the

Henry Ford sits on one of the first 9N tractors to leave the plant in 1939. This was the first tractor to provide farmers with the benefits of the Ferguson three-point hitch system. *Ford Motor Company Photomedia*

work of lifting will be 2,350 Sin 16.7 degrees [equals] 675 pounds.

With 69-inch wheelbase and 19-inch-radius rear wheels, the weight transfer will be 675 [times] 19/69 [equals] 186 pounds transferred from the front to the rear. This figure divided by cosine 16.70 to convert it to its value in a vertical direction becomes 186/.9578 [equals] 194 pounds. This transfer increases with the size of the wheels.

Weight distribution for 30 percent grade with 1,000 pounds draft and 38-inch wheels

	Front	Rear
Original weight without plow	812	1,064
Added weight of plow	308	
Transferred by weight of plow	-168	+168
Transferred by pull of plow	0	0
Transferred by rolling resistance	-90	+90
Added plow suction	0	+200
Transferred by plow suction	-114	+114
Transferred by hill climbing torque	-194	+194
Total [pounds]	246	2,138

Other methods of hitching the implements to the tractor usually apply an upwardly inclined force which lifts part of the implement weight. A certain amount of downward force is needed on some implements so the Ferguson linkage makes lighter implements possible, for it applies a straight-ahead, horizontal pull.

Further Analysis of the System

Another study from August 1939, presumably from Ford Motor Company, also provides detailed analysis of the system and how it works. Remember that in 1939 this system was revolutionary enough that engineers and lay people alike were analyzing and quantifying the system to see if it really did work as Ferguson said it would—and if it could be trusted. Excerpts of the study include these passages:

The plow (Fig. 1) is connected to the tractor through the links AB and CD, producing a parallel lift. The link EF connected from the power lift arm GE to the lower link

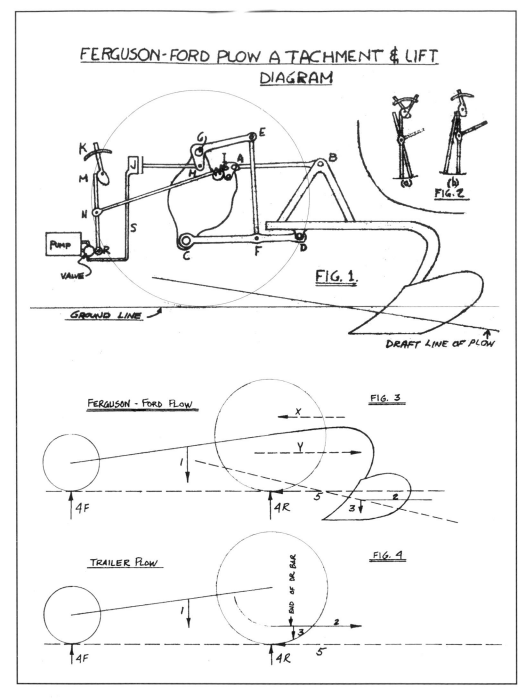

FERGUSON-FORD PLOW ATTACHMENT & LIFT DIAGRAM

FIG. 1.

GROUND LINE

DRAFT LINE OF PLOW

FIG. 2

FERGUSON - FORD PLOW

FIG. 3

TRAILER PLOW

FIG. 4

the pump, though running, is not actually pumping oil.

A. Interaction of Hand and Automatic Control. The lower end of lever MR is connected to the valve V, which, in the various positions:

1. Releases oil to the pump, which forces it into hydraulic cylinder and lifts arms.
2. Locks the oil in the hydraulic cylinder so that arms are fixed in position.
3. Releases oil from the hydraulic cylinder so that lift arms will drop if any downward force (such as weight of plow) is applied to them.
4. Releases oil pressure under certain conditions, acting as a safety device.

The lever MR is floating in that it has no fixed point about which it rotates. The lever is operated (Fig. 2):

1. By the manual control lever K, in which case it turns about point N and thus moves valve V.
2. By plunger NI, in which case it turns about point M and so moves valve V. These motions can take place entirely independent of each other and may operate the valve into any of the positions described in the paragraph above.

B. In Practice:

1. With tractor gears in neutral but power takeoff shaft (driving pump) running, the operator moves hand lever to release oil from hydraulic cylinder, and plow drops to the ground of its own weight. In this position, the plow can be raised off the ground by hand, because the oil control valve is in the open position and oil, therefore, can pass in and out of the hydraulic cylinder freely. A movement of the manual lever in the opposite direction will close the relief passage and open the pump suction so that oil will be forced into the hydraulic cylinder and lift the plow off the ground.
2. (a) With the tractor in gear and moving forward and power takeoff shaft running, the operator moves the hand lever, allowing the plow to drop as in 1. above.

CD raises and lowers the plow under the action of the external power lift arm GE.

The internal lift arm GH is operated by the hydraulic cylinder J which, in turn, is controlled by the combined action of the hand lever K and the rod NI, actuating the valve V, which allows oil to be pumped into cylinder J or released from it. It is to be noted that cylinder J is single acting. It can lift the

plow but cannot push the plow further into the ground. (Cultivators must be so pushed.)

The oil pump P is a four-cylinder plunger pump directly on the power takeoff shaft. It, therefore, operates only when the shaft is turning. The transmission oil itself is used in the lift. The control valve V is on the suction side of the pump, so that when no oil is required in the cylinder J,

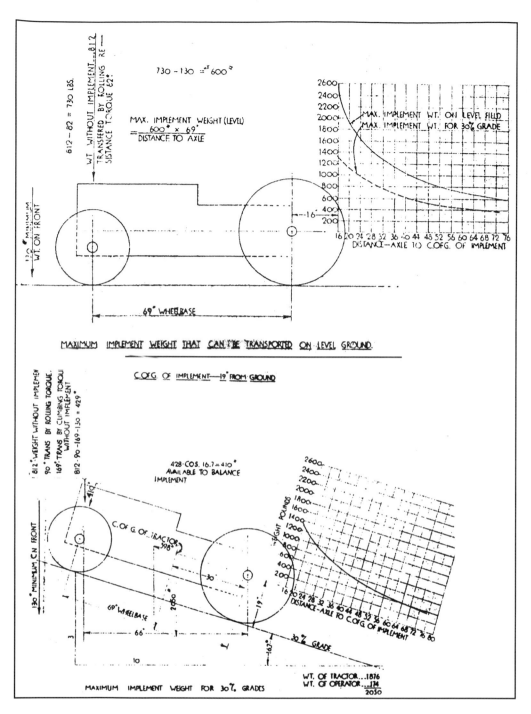

MAXIMUM IMPLEMENT WEIGHT THAT CAN BE TRANSPORTED ON LEVEL GROUND.

C. OF G. OF IMPLEMENT—19" FROM GROUND

MAXIMUM IMPLEMENT WEIGHT FOR 30% GRADES

"A," and the valve will close off the relief passage from hydraulic cylinder, preventing further oil from escaping and so, in turn, preventing the cylinder from allowing plow to drop further.

In an absolutely level field, with absolutely uniform soil, this state of equilibrium will continue as long as the tractor is driven forward at uniform speed and the hand control lever is not moved. It is to be noted that, in this position, the whole mechanism is locked and the plow running at uniform depth.

(b) A variation of the plow draft (under running conditions), due to any cause, will change the compressive force on link AB and so move the plunger NI. This movement will change the amount of oil in the hydraulic cylinder, through operation of valve V, to again produce equilibrium.

For example, if the plow runs into a hard patch, the force in AB will increase, plunger NI will move lever MR toward front of tractor, causing valve V to open pump passage so that pump forces oil into hydraulic cylinder and begins to raise plow. This causes reduction of draft and, therefore, compression in link AB, which allows plunger NI to move toward rear and again close valve V, establishing equilibrium with the plow at a different depth than previously, but with the same drawbar pull.

A return to the former soil condition will reverse this process and the plow will return to the former depth.

(c) Under operating conditions as in (a) above, a movement of the hand lever will:
1. If small, merely set a new point at which plunger NI will automatically establish equilibrium by shifting the plow deeper or shallower, until the correct depth is again obtained. Thus the hand lever position determines the draft that the automatic control will set on the plow. In uniform soil conditions,

In this case, however, due to the forward motion, the plow will enter the ground and begin to exert a draft or "drawbar pull" on the tractor. Because this force is applied to the plowshare which is in the ground and below the links connecting plow and tractor, the effect is to put a tension in link CD and a compression in AB.

The plow will continue to sink into the ground under its weight and downward suck only, building up heavier forces in the links until the compression in link AB rises high enough to compress the spring at I, and so move plunger AI in a forward direction. This will, in turn, move lever MR as described in second paragraph under

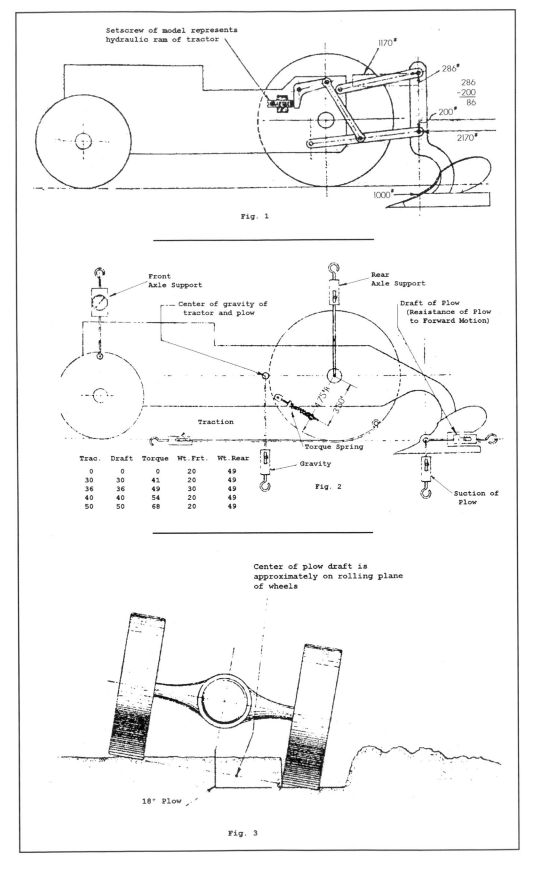

Setscrew of model represents
hydraulic ram of tractor

1170#

286#

$\dfrac{286}{-200}$
$\overline{86}$

200#

2170#

1000#

Fig. 1

Front
Axle Support

Center of gravity of
tractor and plow

Rear
Axle Support

Draft of Plow
(Resistance of Plow
to Forward Motion)

Traction

Torque Spring

Gravity

Suction of
Plow

Fig. 2

Trac.	Draft	Torque	Wt.Frt.	Wt.Rear
0	0	0	20	49
30	30	41	20	49
36	36	49	30	49
40	40	54	20	49
50	50	68	20	49

Center of plow draft is
approximately on rolling plane
of wheels

18" Plow

Fig. 3

this draft-weight gives a uniform depth because the draft will be uniform.

2. If large, move the valve V to a position calling for zero draft on the plow. The plow will then be lifted clear of the ground and will rise to its top position (fully raised) and stay there. Its rise beyond this point is prevented by an internal arrangement which stops the feed of oil to the pump and, at the same time, locks the oil in the lift cylinder to prevent the plow from dropping.

(d) With tractor plowing at a uniform depth, the tractor and plow must be considered as one rigid structure and the following forces are acting on the unit:

1. Weight of tractor and plow.
2. Approximately horizontal component of earth pressure against share.
3. Approximately vertical component of earth pressure against share.
4. Upward pressure of ground on tires.
5. Horizontal traction force of ground against tires.

These forces give exactly the same net effect on the tractor as any directly attached plow, whether rigid or flexible. The difference between the forces here and with a "pull-behind" plow is that the weight of plow and suck of plow in this hook-up both come entirely on the tractor, increasing four at rear and decreasing four at front, so that the rear wheel is capable of more traction.

With the trailer plow, part of the weight and suck are taken by the plow wheels and, therefore, do not add to the pressure of the tractor rear wheels against the ground. There is no less tendency in the integral hook-up to raise the tractor front wheels, because the weight of plow and suck of plow are applied well behind rear axle of tractor and, therefore, tend to lift the tractor front wheels as well as add weight to the rear wheels. (Figure 3).

If forces X and Y acting between plow and tractor through links AB

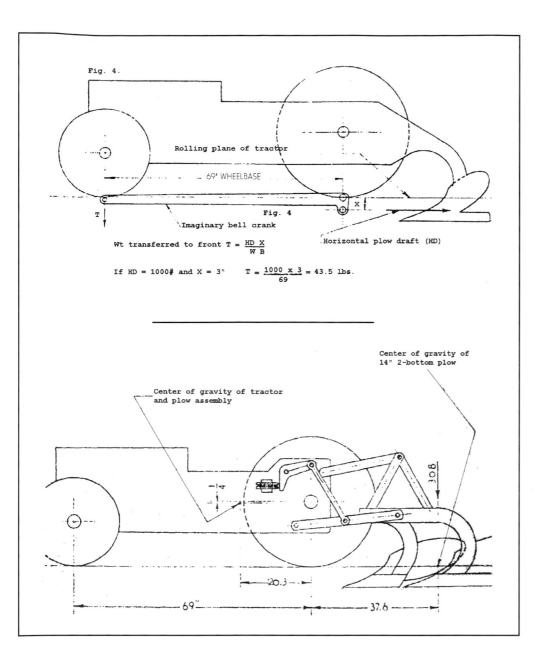

Fig. 4.

Rolling plane of tractor

— 69' WHEELBASE

Fig. 4

Imaginary bell crank

Horizontal plow draft (HD)

Wt transferred to front $T = \dfrac{HD \; X}{WB}$

If HD = 1000# and X = 3" $T = \dfrac{1000 \times 3}{69} = 43.5$ lbs.

Center of gravity of tractor and plow assembly

Center of gravity of 14" 2-bottom plow

30.8

20.3

69"

37.6

and CB are looked at alone, they appear to be causing the tractor to press down harder on its front wheels and less hard on its rear wheels.

These two forces, however, cannot act at all unless 2 is also present— and, therefore, 5—(except as later noted) and these four, with several others not shown, must, therefore, be examined all together as a group of forces acting on the tractor alone. Since, however, X and Y are merely internal stresses in the rigid structure

consisting of plow and tractor, they must be disregarded when considering whether the net effect of the externally applied forces tends to turn the unit over frontward or backward.

On this basis then, it is to be noted that the resultant of 2 and 3 combined must be a normal draft line of a plow as indicated by the sloping dotted line in Figure 3. This line passes above the point of contact of the rear wheel with the ground; therefore, its net effect is to turn the tractor over backward. This

effect is normally counteracted by the weight of the tractor up any rise or hill, just as in the ordinary trailing plow hook-up to proportions that will actually lift the front wheels.

Attaching a trailer plow to a drawbar at a height that leaves the plow wheels taking no load would have identical effect, in normal operation, of the Ferguson hook-up with its integral plow, in respect to the pulling power of the tractor, because there the suck and weight of the plow would be on the tractor.

Such an arrangement would, however, pull the tractor over backward easier than the integral hook-up, because the plowshares would be much further to the rear of the tractor, and consequently, the line of draft would be higher.

Conversely, if in either type the plow bottoms could be moved far enough forward so that the draft line came below the contact point of rear wheel and ground, there would be no tendency to turn tractor over under any circumstances.

C. Special effects:

1. If the tractor front wheels suddenly rise over an obstruction, this will cause the plunger NI to compress its spring and move inward because the plow, projecting as it does behind the rear tractor wheels, would otherwise have to run almost instantaneously deeper.

   This action of NI causes the hydraulic cylinder to lift the plow in relation to the tractor just enough to allow the plow to preserve its uniform depth.

   The dropping of the front tractor wheels into a ditch has the opposite effect on the lift mechanism and results in a level furrow. In the same way, a sudden rise or fall of the rear tractor wheels leaves the plow riding at uniform depth.

2. If the draft of the plow rises in operations more rapidly than the operation of the lift can relieve it raising the plow,

The purpose of this leaflet is to show the wide array of implements that can be utilized on just about every farm, including when the field work is all done.

or if the operator set the manual control too deep, the tractor wheels will finally slip. This reduces the draft to nearly zero, and, since the horizontal forces in AB and CD depend on draft, they also drop to nearly zero.

This allows spring on plunger NI to move the latter to rear of tractor, shutting off the pump from the lift, and moving valve to the locked position. The weight of the tractor will then be supported on its front wheels and the plow through the lower link, and the lift link EF, which now acts as a rigid structure, since the weight of the tractor is not great enough to again open the control

valve through compressing the spring on plunger.

The wheels will continue to run "slipping" and causing a slight draft on the plow. If the wheels are stopped and the draft thus dropped to zero, the tractor will settle down on its rear wheels so that traction in reverse can be obtained and the plow backed up. If the manual control lever is operated to lift the plow, this will also give traction, and, if the plow is not otherwise prevented, it will lift out of the ground.

3. If the plow hooks under a root or stone too strong to be moved, the tractor will either stall or the wheels will slip in second gear. If in low gear, and the wheels can get traction, the front wheels of the tractor will be lifted off the ground even more than with the conventional hook-up, because the power lift will come into action if the wheels continue to turn.

This will, however, finally compress the plunger spring to such an extent that the hydraulic control valve overruns its working positions and releases the oil from the lift cylinder, allowing the front end to drop to the ground.

This is a safety feature incorporated in the Ferguson lift. It is almost impossible to turn over backward any tractor with rubber tires, on account of lack of traction. It is quite impossible to actually turn over backward any tractor with integral plow.

D. Power Takeoff and Pulley:

1. Since the power lift pump is driven directly off the power takeoff shaft, the latter must be running if the lift is to be used. The belt pulley is also driven from the power takeoff shaft. The power takeoff shaft can be declutched as in other tractors, and the same clutch puts power lift out of action. The power lift can be made inoperative also by pushing manual lever all the way forward. This leaves control valve open so that no oil is circulated to the lift.

Three-Point System Terminology

Unit principle: The close coupling of implement with the tractor, making the two a single unit.

Depth wheel: A three-point implement was attached to and carried by the tractor. So, it needed no wheels. This made for some early and continuing problems concerning controlling the working depth of the implement. Early designs before draft control was perfected were fitted with a small wheel that rode in the furrow bottom to help control working depth.

Duplex hitch: Two-point linkage that used two parallel links, one above the other.

Floating skid: Rear skid that rode the bottom of the furrow and linked to the hitch point of the tractor. As the rear tractor wheel either raised or lowered, the tractor transferred weight to the rear skid that adjusted the plow depth.

Hydraulic draft control: Amount of draft required is sensed through the sensing link, and the hydraulic pump response is to either raise or lower working depth of implement accordingly.

Overload release: Automatic release of hydraulic pressure to protect the implement if an obstruction is hit.

Suction side control: Hydraulic pump is supplied on input side when sensing link activates pump. This eliminated aeration of fluid and jerky motion of lift links.

Lower-link sensing: The first duplex hitch had the lower link attached to the hydraulic pump sensing unit.

Virtual hitch point: The dynamics of a hitching arrangement that causes the line of draft of an implement to originate from a point other than where it is connected to the tractor.

Draft: The act, effort, or force of pulling a load.

Draft control: This is a systems design that automatically regulates—stabilizes—the implement working depth by the amount of draft—effort—required to pull the implement through the soil.

Weight transfer: This is the condition where the weight of the plow itself plus the downward force created by the suction of the plow or implement into the soil is transferred to the rear tractor tires. It works in reverse, too. Since the unit principle imparts the weight of the tractor to the plow, the plow doesn't need to be heavy to achieve penetration.

Flow-on-demand system: This is the same principle as suction side control.

Check chains/antisway blocks: These are chains attached to the two lower arms of the three-point linkage that allow lateral movement when the implement is engaged, but limit sway when the implement is raised.

An early dealer sign championed "Wheel-less implements" in a day when all other farm equipment needed wheels in order to function.

CHAPTER FIVE

Plows

DESIGN, DEVELOPMENT, & MANUFACTURE

Move that dirt and make it fly! This tractor breaks up a stand of alfalfa with a rare English-built Ferguson quarter-turn reversible plow. In England, these plows are often called "butterfly" plows. This is a Type 60-AC, which is the same as a Type T-AG-28. This plow allows the operator to throw dirt in just one direction. It's well-suited for hillsides where it's desirable to turn all furrows uphill to combat erosion, small plots where waste areas such as dead furrows are to be eliminated, building terraces, and irrigated fields where the land must be kept level.

T he handshake agreement is understood to mean that Henry Ford was to manufacture the tractor with a three-point hydraulic system. Harry Ferguson was to handle manufacturing of the implements as well as sales and distribution of both.

There may be some debate about who contributed most to the tractor design. However, there's no argument about who manufactured the tractor and where it was manufactured. Things aren't as clear-cut when it comes to the implements, though. But when you're building farm tractors, a tractor without implements is of little value. This was doubly so with the new three-point hydraulic system, because the tractor didn't perform well without its accompanying specially designed implements.

According to the report, "Harry Ferguson, Inc., Tractor and Implement Sales in Quantities," tractors accounted for 55 percent of total dollar sales volume. The implements supplied 45 percent. From this, and the fact it was hard to sell the tractor without its specialized implements, tractors and implements were approximately equally important to the program.

The Ford team of engineers did a remarkable job of getting the tractor into production. In fact, tractor production occasionally outstripped implement production to the point that the tractor line was shut down until enough implements could be provided.

Here's what many Ford owners consider the classic, best-looking three-point hitch plow of all time: The 14-inch, two-bottom Dearborn plow.

In the early years, sales outstripped production of both tractors and implements. This gives testimony to the increasing acceptance and surging popularity of the implements and tractors as well as the abilities of both Ford and Ferguson. Ford and his staff were production-oriented, while Ferguson and his organization did their best at selling the product.

Records of the development and production of implements are far more fragmented than that of tractor production. The bulk of the available records concerning implement development were gathered by the legal staffs of both companies in preparation for the lawsuit that occurred after the split between the two principals. Both sides gathered documents, records, and personal interviews to support their positions. There are substantial records that help to identify just where and when the implements came on line and who developed them.

In the complaint filed in the District Court of the United States for the Southern District of New York, January 8, 1948, plaintiffs Harry Ferguson and Harry Ferguson, Inc., state in allegation 44 that:

"Implements were procured by Ferguson Company from a number of different manufacturers and were distributed and sold by the Ferguson Company. Ford Motor Company did not have anything to do with the design, procurement, distribution, or sale of the implements, except that Ford Motor Company produced plows in accordance with Ferguson's designs and specifications and exclusively for sale to the Ferguson Company until such manufacture was discontinued in 1944."

This statement highlights the fact that Ferguson wasn't a manufacturer. The early firm of Ferguson-Sherman Manufacturing, Inc., didn't produce implements. Instead, it procured them from other manufacturers. Probably the reason "Manufacturing" was included in the name was a carryover from the Ferguson-Sherman company of Evansville, Indiana, where Eber and George did produce the duplex plow for the Fordson. Perhaps they envisioned actually manufacturing some three-point implements later on. The above legal document excerpt shows that not only did Ford produce the tractors, but the plows were also produced by the Ford Motor Company until 1944.

The Primary Players

Tractor development and production was located at the Ford Motor Company Rouge plant in Michigan. The engineering offices and the area where most of the planning was done was called the "Blue Room." According to a January 1951 document drafted by Ford Motor Company, the Ford personnel operating in this room were:

- Henry Ford—A direct participant, in overall charge.
- C. E. Sorensen—Next in line to Ford, general supervisor.
- L. S. Sheldrick—In charge of the design project.
- Howard Simpson—Worked on plow design and tread width adjustment until early 1939. Head designer until his resignation in February 1939.
- Mark Freeley—Succeeded Simpson as head designer, directly supervised Ford engineering and drafting personnel.

In Howard Simpson's two volumes of *Reminiscences*, he recalled that Sherman and Ferguson had moved into offices at the Rouge near his office and came to visit. Also Willie Sands and John Chambers, Ferguson employees, worked much of the time in the same room with him, but weren't working under his direction. Simpson commented on the Ferguson plow:

The plow that Ferguson brought over in 1939 [Author's note: He surely meant 1938.] was in a rough condition. It was made out of bent solid bars. Where they drilled holes through it made weak spots. This plow was not acceptable to Mr. Ford and I redesigned it also. I did all that work myself. I made up all the drawings. I was the only one working on it. That plow was a blacksmith's job and was not designed for volume production.

On November 25, 1938, Simpson noted:

I have now been at the Rouge two weeks and Mr. Ford had been down every day to con-

"Mr. Ferguson Plow Man" Gene Kruse, Lincoln, Nebraska, believes he owns more different models of Ferguson plows than anyone in the world. Here he is with his 13 plows. Twelve of these plows are three-point, and one used with the Fordson tractor is the predecessor of the three-point system.

fer with me on the Ferguson tractor. I had wood models made up of plowshares and frames which they seemed to be more interested in than the tractor at the moment. The first plowshare model we made, Sorensen said, was a son-of-a-bitch thing.

However, I made the thing up the way he had wanted it. It would be hard to cast. . . . Between then and during the months of December and January, I was continually sketching up models of plows and cultivators and I did some work on the tractor also.

Ferguson practiced a system of diversified manufacturing. He believed in many suppliers providing parts for any one implement. The reason he followed this program may have had to do with possible labor unrest and the idea that a strike at one location therefore couldn't completely stop production of implements.

And, as in the case of the middlebuster, for example, the suppliers and assembly point were located in the southern part of the country to lessen freight costs. This was also practiced in regard to certain West Coast implements. This

This Dearborn plow made in 1947, a Type 10-1, was one of the first out the door carrying the Dearborn name. While the later plows have an offset three-point arm, this early model instead features an adjustable cam that allows the angle of tilt to be varied. However, when used in the field, vibration caused the cam to turn on its own. Dearborn's remedy was to change to the solid arm.

system had a downside, however. It was paper-work-intense and difficult to oversee from a main office in Detroit that was directly responsible to Harry Ferguson in England.

The Shermans' Integral Roles

Some of the key personnel involved in the procurement department of the Ferguson group obviously included the Sherman brothers. Before there was much of a Ferguson organization at Detroit, George Sherman did most of the work to line up suppliers for the implements. Eber Sherman held the Fordson tractor distributorship for the entire Unites States in the 1920s. His contracts were invaluable to Ferguson in setting up the dealership network for the new tractor and implements. It doesn't appear that Eber spent time actually helping with the development of the tractor and implements. But this is due, no doubt, to his efforts to bring dealers into the Ferguson-Sherman network.

Eber noted in his letter to Henry Ford that he'd been in Salt Lake City talking with dealers, Fordson dealers no doubt, that could be brought into the Ferguson-Sherman fold of distributors and dealers.

It was probably George Sherman who first made contact with Roger Kyes of Empire Plow Company when he was working to establish that company as a supplier of cultivator parts. Sherman was so impressed with Kyes' knowledge of the implement business that he recom-

mended that Ferguson retain Kyes as a consultant. The friction that later arose between the Shermans and Ferguson in 1941 provided an opportunity for Kyes to install himself as president of the Ferguson organization and remove the Shermans. Even after that event, the Shermans didn't disappear completely.

Merritt Hill was an executive and officer of Harry Ferguson, Inc., from 1941 until July 1946, and during that time was director of procurement from 1942 to 1944. Hill left Ferguson in early 1947 to become Dearborn's chief sales executive. It

was Hill who pointed out that the plow is the most important item in an implement line. He estimated that the Ferguson company sold one moldboard plow for almost every tractor sold between 1939 and 1942. During most of this time, according to Hill, Ford manufactured or procured and supplied to Ferguson all service parts for the plows, except a comparatively few special types of shares.

These few special shares were purchased by Ford directly from David Bradley Manufacturing Company of Bradley, Illinois. Sometime before 1940, Bradley was absorbed by Sears, Roebuck & Company and joined its manufacturing divisions. Bradley was a supplier for other plow manufacturers, such as Oliver and Allis-Chalmers. The firm had a production capacity of approximately 900,000 shares a year in 1948. It's believed that Ferguson owned the special tooling at Bradley for making his plowshares. At this time, it was standard practice for the buyer to either own outright or pay for the tooling on an amortized basis.

A massive implement, this three-bottom disc plow has 26-inch serrated blades. Originally offered as a two-bottom unit, a third bottom could be added as an option.

In either case, once the tooling was paid for, the buyer could ask for, and receive, the tooling once the contract between the companies was fulfilled. Such tooling could be quite expensive, occasionally in excess of $500,000.

During this time Bradley also supplied Ferguson's standard plow bases. These were purchased directly by Ford and assembled at the Rouge plant.

This arrangement for plow production continued between Ford and Ferguson until sometime in 1944 or 1945. Plow production ceased for undisclosed reasons, probably because Ford didn't want to be in the implement manufacturing business, or he wanted to free up manufacturing space for war contracts. Also, Ferguson always believed that the prices Ford charged for its plows were too high. For that reason, Ferguson began to seek other manufacturers for plows as early as 1942.

Ferguson Seeks a Source for Plows

A memorandum from Hill to Kyes in January 1943 stated:

This three-bottom disc plow from the early 1950s, Type PA 021, has nonserrated blades. The third bottom was an add-on option for this plow if the farmer traded up to a more-powerful tractor. This disc plow was ideal for mixing heavy surface trash with soil, constructing and maintaining terraces, working heavy or wet soils that don't scour easily, plowing in fields infested with stones or roots, and for penetrating hard-packed soils.

At this time we are attempting to find a satisfactory source of supply for making the plows which Ford has been making, and in order to get anyone to tool up and take over this responsibility it will be necessary to guarantee at least a 2,000-unit run for 1943, and there is a fair possibility that many additional plows will be needed anyway.

Several companies were approached, including B. F. Avery & Sons, David Bradley Manufacturing Co., and the Clark Grave Vault Company of Columbus, Ohio. The Clark Grave Vault Company was an interesting and costly venture for the Ferguson group. Just why procurement people from a farm implement concern would approach a company specializing in vault manufacturing is unclear. However, Clark did hold some war contracts and perhaps it was looking to diversify after the war. The company seemed willing to pursue the Ferguson business. Unfortunately, the plow proved much different from its existing production processes, and quality and quantity difficulties caused Ferguson to discontinue its plow program at the Clark company before even one plow was produced.

However, great amounts of money and time were spent on tooling. Clark threatened to sue Ferguson, and Ferguson paid out approximately $500,000 in settlement of claims for tooling expenses and other losses.

"No way but up" would be an apt description of the plow business from Ferguson's viewpoint. And things did improve when negotiations opened with the Budd Company in 1944. This Detroit firm had substantial contracts with the auto industry and was well-versed in fabricated steel production. Its products included automobile bodies, doors, fenders, and hoods for the "Big Three" auto manufacturers. It also built railroad cars, naval equipment, and aircraft parts.

As of 1947, the Budd Company was a consolidation of two separate firms, Budd Manufacturing Company and Budd Wheel Company. These companies had joint total assets in excess of $35,000,000 and sales of roughly $47,000,000.

After the Budd Company was satisfied that Ferguson had a satisfactory relationship with Ford, it jumped into the plow business. In

October 1944, Budd agreed to manufacture plow frames for Ferguson, who placed a formal order for 20,000 plows. Actual production in 1945 was 34,000 units.

Negotiations were also under way with a company called Farm Tools of Evansville, Indiana. This eventually resulted in production of plow bases at the rate of 250 a day.

Records indicate that Ford produced the complete plow (with the exception of some of the more specialized plowshares). So when Ferguson began buying plow frames and plow bases from other companies, it was necessary to find a source for plow coulter assemblies. The coulter assembly includes a check chain, a jointer for scraping earth from the blade or disc, and the jointer arm. Also needed to complete the plow is a furrow wheel assembly.

For this procurement, Ferguson sought the French & Hecht Co. of Davenport, Iowa, in April 1944. Because this wasn't considered a large or vital item, it's likely the orders were simply handled with a purchase order serving as the entire contract. Again, following Ferguson's

44

established practice, the parts were shipped directly to the Budd Company for final assembly on the plow unit.

Plow demands were escalating as sales of the 2N tractor increased. In the first six months of 1943, Ferguson bought 1,622 plows from Ford. During the same period one year later, the number rose to 12,597. During the first year that plows were manufactured at the Budd Company, production figures reached 34,000. In 1946, production records show a total of 43,000 units manufactured.

The First Signs of Discord

Ferguson had two good years before the impending rift between Ford and Ferguson cast an uncertain shadow over production of all implements. There's some evidence that as early as 1942, Ferguson began approaching other manufacturers for production of what he considered "his" tractor.

Yet letters between Ferguson and Ford always reflected a most cordial and respectful relationship between the two men. This feeling was undoubtedly genuine. However, Ferguson was, as Henry Ford II put it, "A most difficult man to deal with in business matters."

Diaries and correspondence relating to the early tractor and plow production substantiate that Ferguson had the last word on quality control of the units. Routinely, after the Ford people had approved production for

This 180-degree roll-over plow carries four 14-inch bottoms. It relies on a mechanical linkage to rotate the plows. The operator pulls the handle to release the pins after raising the plow out of the ground. This allows the plow to roll over for the return trip, tossing dirt in the same direction.

45

Although sporting a hefty 16-inch bottom, it was by design that there was only one bottom to this plow. This is the plow for the heavy, clay-type soils that soak up horsepower, especially when set to plow deeply. It's also excellent at covering trash.

shipment, Ferguson would reject many of the tractors and plows. This resulted in substantial reworking and refitting before he would release them, which was understandably a constant source of tension and frustration for both the Ford and Ferguson staffs.

This situation was understandable because of Ferguson's almost obsessive pursuit of perfection. He wasn't production-oriented, and he could never appreciate the Ford position and experience in running a manufacturing operation. Ferguson, however, had legitimate concerns about quality. A study by an outside firm reported much of Ford's tooling for the tractors and implements was outdated, in disrepair, and unable to hold the necessary tolerance required. A second possible reason for Ferguson's desire to take production of the tractor elsewhere was his concern over cost and pricing, both of which he considered excessive on Ford's part.

After the war Henry Ford II looked at the tractor operation and concluded that Ford Motor Company was losing money on every tractor it manufactured and on every N-Series tractor it had ever produced. He proposed that Ford Motor Company take over Harry Ferguson's marketing and distribution company. The deal would give Ford 70 percent and Ferguson 30 percent. The response was predictable: Ferguson would have none of it.

After six years the "handshake agreement" was over. It left Ford with a tractor, but no implement, while Ferguson had the implements, but no tractor. Ferguson set about the difficult task of either finding a U.S. tractor manufacturer or starting up his own plant from scratch. The only plus on his side of the ledger was the tractor production in England that was under way with a tractor design and all the blueprints and specs.

Ford, on the other hand, knew which suppliers were already manufacturing exactly the implements they needed to sell with their tractors, but getting them on board would be a challenge. That's because Ferguson had the suppliers of big-ticket items signed into exclusive rights contracts that invariably required a one-year notice from either party before the contract could be broken. In addition, many of the implements were either covered by patents held by the Ferguson com-

Arguably the most beautiful—or ugly—of all the three-point hitch plows is what American farmers know as the quarter-turn roll-over plow. It's called the "Butterfly" plow in England for obvious reasons. It has dual single 16-inch bottoms. While most roll-over plows built to throw dirt in one direction rotate 180 degrees, this Type T-AO-28 plow is unique in going over only 90 degrees or so.

Here's another quarter-turn plow. Without dead furrows with which to contend, it's well-adapted to irrigation farming. However, this plow can also be quite effective in plowing up terraces and in maintaining contour farming.

47

Implement Identification System

It's helpful to understand as much as possible about the model numbering system that was used, or in the case of the Ferguson implements, the numbers and letters utilized instead of model numbers. Both the Ferguson implement and the Dearborn implement identification systems were evolutionary, as these examples of a 1939 purchase order illustrate:

10A-AO	10-inch two-bottom general-purpose plow
10B-AO	10-inch two-bottom sod or clay plow
12A-AO	12-inch two-bottom general-purpose plow
12B-AO	12-inch two-bottom sod or clay plow
14A-AO	14-inch two-bottom general-purpose plow
14B-AO	14-inch two-bottom sod or clay plow
16A-AO	16-inch single-bottom general-purpose plow
16B-AO	16-inch single-bottom sod or clay plow

Obviously the first numbers correspond to the plow furrow width, 10, 12, 14, and 16 inches.

The next letter consistently matches with the type of bottom: "A" for general purpose, and "B" for sod- or clay-type bottom. The "1950 Ferguson Moldboard Plow operating and assembly instructions" help round out the picture: The type marked on plowshares along with a code breakdown help to understand the system.

The first whole number indicates width of cut, and the first letter indicates type of bottom. On shares, the next letter indicates the material from which the share is constructed. The third letter identifies it as a plow or plow part. Finally, the fourth letter indicates made in the United States.

Keep in mind that the system was constantly being revised and added to as the line of implements grew. However the basics were consistent. Of course, this system was changed when Dearborn Motors began marketing the implements. In the Dearborn system of model numbers, the prefix number 10 specified ground-breaking implements. The following numbers identified the type of implement.

For example, 10-89 was the number for the subsoiler that was sold only as a complete unit in contrast plows. Plows would have a frame, cross-shaft, front base, rear base, tail wheel, coulters, and jointers.

There is no such item as a stock plow. When the dealer ordered a plow, it was similar to ordering a basic auto and then adding the extra options. With the plow, all the numbers after the 10 prefix specified the options, such as type of bottoms needed, the width of shear, the type of shear, and the moldboard style. The 10 prefix included the Dearborn Tillit as well as disc plows.

At some point the whole small line was called the 101 series. A suffix number was added to the 10 to form a three-digit list of 10 plus a number that would constitute the complete plow. However, a dealer could still "custom design" a plow for his customer by ordering any 10 prefix plus components to construct the desired type of plow.

Prefix 11	Numbers included all soil-fitting implements such as disc harrows and spring-tooth harrows.
Prefix 12	Included corn planters, as well as grain drills.
Prefix 13	Covered all types of cultivators and rotary hoes.
Prefix 14	Specified haying machinery, balers, mowers, forage harvesters, and grain and forage blowers.
Prefix 15	Open. This prefix was to be applied to implements or accessories as they were developed.
Prefix 16	Included combines and corn pickers.
Prefix 17	Open.
Prefix 18	Open.
Prefix 19	Identified material-handling implements loaders, scoops, and blades.
Prefix 20	Includes manure and lime spreaders.
Prefix 21	Wagons.
Prefix 22	Rotary cutters.

As time went on, and more so as Dearborn Motors was taken over by Ford, it went factory direct to its dealers with the three-digit ID number. A suffix was used for the complete line, but subcomponents were still in the ordering system.

This is on an early Ferguson-Sherman Manufacturing Corporation identification plate that was made in the United States. The plate identifies it as a Type 12B plow. Deciphered, that means it's a 12-inch, two-bottom sod-or-clay plow. Regardless of the name on the identification plate, until 1944 Ford designed and made all the plows for the 9N tractor.

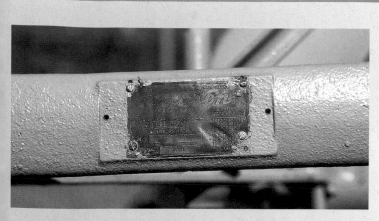

The Type 14A is an early Ferguson-Sherman Manufacturing Corporation plow with a 14-inch, two-bottom general purpose plow.

The Dearborn post-hole digger's support arm proudly proclaims it as a product from the Ford Tractor Division, Birmingham, Michigan. However, credit for manufacturing this Model 22-11 goes to Danuser Machine Company.

Equipment made by Carrington Terracer Company, Fulton, Missouri, carries a Harry Ferguson, Inc., Detroit, Michigan, identification plate.

pany, or Ferguson held a license agreement with the vendors that gave him the exclusive right to use the vendor's patents covering implement design. Exclusive rights contracts and patent contracts notwithstanding, Ford looked for an opening to tap the ready supply of implements. Second only in importance to the implements was the distribution network of dealers that the Ferguson company had developed. This, too, was targeted by the Ford camp. This confrontation over implement suppliers and dealers brought out the best and the worst of both parties.

This is also a transitional point for tracking the genealogy of the three-point implements of U.S. origin. Up to this point, the implements carried either a Ferguson-Sherman or a Harry Ferguson, Inc., identification plate, regardless of the actual manufacturer. In some cases, these ID plates also carried the name of the actual manufacturing company.

Note that this pertains only to the implements sold through one or the other of Harry Ferguson's companies. There were many other manufacturers from large firms such as Sears, Roebuck & Company to small blacksmith shops that were either making or adapting implements to fit the three-point system.

Word of the Split Gets Out

In early 1946, rumors were widespread of the impending split between Ford and Ferguson, and it takes little imagination to picture the confusion among the distributors and dealerships. They were wondering if they'd have product to sell and parts for machinery already in the field. Even greater concern was found at the manufacturing companies. Most of them had a high-dollar investment in tooling and raw materials, not to mention work in progress and finished inventory. They also had to consider their workforces and overhead. Most, if not all, such vendors worked from a yearly production order generated by Harry Ferguson that was always released in the fall.

Questions that arose included: If Ford stopped making tractors for Ferguson, would Ferguson take delivery of the implements, and if he took delivery, could he pay for them?

The Budd Company was the first to feel the impact of the two companies scrambling

Budd: Caught in the Middle

for advantage. That Budd was vital to both parties for plows is indicated by the investment Budd made in its plow venture. The company's goal for postwar production was $7,000,000 in annual gross sales. It even bought a separate property at which to manufacture plows, and had a capital investment of at least $750,000 before the first plows came off the line.

Budd also had to remake the tooling from the disastrous Clark Grave Vault Company, tooling that Ferguson owned and shipped to Budd. This retooling cost $400,000, which the company billed to Ferguson. New tooling might have been cheaper, but it couldn't have been brought on line as quickly. Ferguson agreed to pay for all tooling necessary for plow production at Budd, so his investment, separate from design and blueprints, was in excess of $1,000,000.

In the spring of 1946, Roger Kyes, president of Harry Ferguson, Inc., was convinced that Ford was going to withdraw from furnishing tractors to Ferguson. He strongly advised cutting back on all implement orders even though there was great demand for certain items, especially plows. Many farmers had purchased tractors with the promise that implements would be delivered soon. The shortage of plows resulted when plow production left the Ford Rouge plant and never got under way at Clark company.

Ignoring the plow shortage, Kyes reduced the orders to the Budd Company for the first half of 1947 to only 5,000 units. E. A. Clark, vice president of Budd, rightly suspected something was afoot and called Ford's Ernie Breech, whom he had known for several years. Clark questioned Breech about the Ford-Ferguson relationship and if Ferguson had cut back on tractor orders. Clark was especially concerned about committing for materials that were difficult to procure. Clark came away from the conversation convinced that regardless of which way the Ford-Ferguson relationship evolved, he'd still have a plow customer.

At the same time, Ford Motor Company was carefully making projections concerning supply, sales, and distribution of a wholly Ford tractor and implement line. As for a plow manufacturer, Ford had no doubts that Budd would supply the plows. A large ace in the hole for the Ford-Budd relationship was the $30,000,000 worth of annual auto-related business that Ford gave Budd. Another favorable factor for Ford was that Ferguson and Budd didn't have a formal contract. It's not known exactly why Fergu-

Made in England, these quarter-turn plows are generally more popular there than in the United States. This one carries the identification plate of Type 60-AE, which is the same as Type T-AG-28, according to the restorer.

This is the plow to locate and restore. Why? Because it's an early two-bottom Ferguson plow. Among the features that distinguish it from later models are the cast top pieces. Also, the rolling coulter pieces are cast right into the main beam rather than as separate brackets, as was done later.

This early two-bottom Ferguson plow, a Type 12-B, is a rare 12-incher. Most such plows had 14-inch bottoms.

son didn't follow his usual business practice with Budd. Perhaps he was so desperate for plows that he didn't want to press the issue.

In December 1946, the Budd Company's Clark reached some decisions. Because Ferguson was Budd's Number One plow customer, Budd wouldn't infringe upon Ferguson's patents or use its tools in making plows for Ford. But Budd could supply both Ferguson and Ford with plows. Budd's business ethics also prohibited it from using Ferguson blueprints for Dearborn production. The company insisted that Dearborn or Ford design a plow and furnish Budd with blueprints, models, and manufacturing specifications.

As a business that had long served as a supplier to auto manufacturers, Budd understood the likelihood of patent problems unless it took certain precautions, and thus insisted that Dearborn furnish prints and specs. Budd didn't want to build a Dearborn plow based on converging linkage, but was comfortable with the proposed parallel linkage. Other points of concern were the A frames, the cross-shaft adjustment assemblies, and the furrow wheels.

Getting around the Patents

To circumvent the Ferguson patents on the crank-shaped cross-shaft, Dearborn's experimental plow models were equipped with a straight 1 1/2-

inch shaft. Ferguson's shaft was 1 3/4-inch and shaped somewhat like a crank. Dearborn engineered a cross-shaft adjuster and U-bolt to compensate for the downward curve in the furrow side of the shaft that was necessary in order for the plow to trail level.

The patented Ferguson "flexible furrow wheel" was replaced by a fixed furrow wheel of Budd design.

Ferguson's A frame was constructed of separate pieces of high carbon steel. Dearborn instead opted for price-reducing, appearance-altering, A-shaped metal stampings.

Archival documents in the Henry Ford Museum & Greenfield Village in Dearborn, Michigan, support the consensus that the Dearborn plows

were essentially a Ferguson design modified to avoid Ferguson plow patents and to economize production. These same documents, mostly compiled for the later court case, contain interesting, although not conclusive, evidence that plow blueprints were traced, erased, and otherwise apparently converted from Ferguson blueprints to serve other purposes.

After testing at Dearborn's test facilities, these types and sizes of plow bases were adopted:
- 14-inch general-purpose two-bottom (L. B. Cockshutt type).
- 12-inch two-bottom plow (Ferguson type).
- 10-inch two-bottom plow (Massey-Harris type).

- 16-inch single-bottom plow (Oliver type).
- 14-inch two-bottom plow (S. B. Cockshutt type).

Plow design was far enough along by March to allow Dearborn to issue a plow order to Budd stating the estimated requirements for the last six months of 1947. This order covered these 40,000 units:

- 18,400 14-inch R two-bottom general-purpose plows.
- 10,400 12-inch two-bottom plows.
- 4,000 10-inch two-bottom plows.
- 4,000 16-inch single-bottom plows.
- 3,200 14-inch S two-bottom plows.

Red plows with both Ford and Dearborn names on an identification plate affixed to the left-hand stamping of the A frame were on the way to still-somewhat-confused distributors, dealers, and farmers. Confusion resulted because the Budd production lines weren't running. Not all the tooling was switched or reworked yet for the Dearborn plow. Records suggest that Budd at

Here's the best way to identify an early Ferguson two-bottom plow, according to restorers: The left side of the tail wheel is completely smooth. Later versions had four rivets protruding slightly. Only in 1941 were smooth tail wheels manufactured and installed on the Type 14-A plows.

The common belief is that Ford wanted to get its name on the early Ferguson two-bottom plows, too, so it had "Ford" in flowing script put in the casting for the main beam. This—perhaps surprisingly—is not true. Even though this is a Ferguson plow, company records conclusively show that it was designed by Ford and built until 1944 by Ford.

Although it's rigged in a side-mount, this Ferguson disc terracer works on the three-point hitch. It's a Type LD O51.

Call it a disc plow or a disc tiller. Regardless, it took a good bit of power to operate this type P-B-20. This unit was made in Canada.

this time was still running production of about 250 to 300 units a day for the Ferguson company.

A red plow hadn't yet reached the end of the production line when a Dearborn meeting of distributors was planned for May 14–15, 1947. Circumstances surrounding a Budd request for 16-inch and 14-inch Ferguson plow frames from dealers suggest that these were reworked to Dearborn designs, painted red, and exhibited at the distributor meeting.

No wonder dealers and distributors were confused and concerned about the supply of tractors and implements that may or may not be available to a hungry market.

Settling on the Shares

Another plow item that was out-sourced by both Ferguson and Dearborn was the plowshare. Shares weren't covered by any patent, so this didn't pose a problem for either company. There were really only a couple of problems that needed to be overcome in regard to the plowshares, most importantly, one of proper fit. It's important that the share face join smoothly to the moldboard face when the share is bolted onto the base.

According to an interview with Harold Brock, this was a problem encountered in 1939 when Ford was developing a plow for Ferguson.

"We produced it [plow] at the Ford factory," Brock said, "and, that was quite a problem, too, because Ferguson was very meticulous in what he wanted, irrespective of what it would cost. So he told us where they [moldboard and share] bolted together. You have just a little line there.

"He said that has to be so exact that you can't feel the line, so we'd have to grind. We had to buy a contour grinder in order to put the share and the board together and grind them so that you didn't find the little connection between them.

Made in England where the soils are generally clayish, this 10-inch, two-bottom plow has longer moldboards that enable them to turn the slice of soil on edge. This allows more aeration and eventual crumbling of soil. It also features an aftermarket adjustment handle that the operator can use to vary the front furrow width while on the move. This is a Type 10 H-AE-28 plow.

"So it was a very precision-made plow. We knew nothing about the need for it. We just accepted his statement that was necessary."

A second problem was being able to provide enough types of shares to make a reasonably complete line for the different soil conditions found throughout the country. Old-line implement manufacturers such as Deere & Company at this time offered as many as 150 different bases and shares.

In contrast, the 1940 Ferguson brochure lists only general-purpose, sod or clay, salt, blackland, Scotch, and chilled bases. Shares available were new Ford cast steel, solid forged steel, chilled cast iron, and soft center.

Pittsburgh Forgings Company, Detroit, Michigan, supplied the moldboards for some, if not all, plows.

The David Bradley Manufacturing Co. was the initial supplier of shares during production at the Ford Rouge plant. However, Ford designed and cast at least one type of share during the hectic start-up period.

"So, what we did was to design a very uniform stressed beam to be made out of cast steel," Brock said. "We had a foundry making cast steel at the time as well as making iron. Cast steel strength wasn't any higher really than rerolled rail steel. But by

making it out of cast steel, you could form it to the shape necessary to use minimum weight.

"And, so we made those plows very light. And we made the bottom and the share out of cast steel as well."

The two main types of shares obtained from Bradley were the solid steel and soft center steel shares. In 1946, Ferguson bought approximately 350,000 such shares from Bradley.

For chilled iron shares, the supplier was Lynchburg Plow Works, an old-line company with an excellent reputation. The number of chilled iron shares was probably less than 10,000 for the year 1946. The first completed Dearborn plows from the Budd factory were shipped in August 1947.

With two 14-inch bottoms, this type of plow has what's often called "Scottish" bottoms. Its specialty is breaking up grassland or sod-bound soils.

Although this plow can only put one bottom into the ground at a time, it's a big, heavy plow, a 180-degree roll-over plow with dual 16-inch bottoms. Lindeman Power Equipment Company made this Type LP-16TW plow.

Ford used these photographs in advertising. This was a single-bottom roll-over plow probably destined for use on an irrigated farm.

When the going gets tough, well, the tough hitch up a Ferguson plow with two 14-inch slatted bottoms. The plow pulls with less drag through the soil since there's not as much moldboard surface area to create friction. A perfect place to use it is in soils that virtually refuse to scour with conventional moldboards.

Krause Corporation made a successful three-point hitch disc plow—although most farmers called it a "one-way" or "one-way plow." The company's first such units often wouldn't track straight when working in extremely dry soils. The addition of a stabilizer bar from the right rear three-point connection to under the axle solved this problem.

F "8" One-Way Disc Plow
FOR FORD AND FERGUSON TRACTORS

INSTRUCTION MANUAL

Krause Corporation, Hutchinson, Kansas, built a highly popular three-point "one-way" or disc plow. Notice that the Krause Corporation instruction manual cover illustrates one of the unit's advantages without mentioning that it could work the ground quite close to a fence line. The inside pages give instructions both with visuals and text to ensure that new users get the most from their purchases.

CHAPTER SIX

Cultivators, Tillers, and Middlebusters

DEARBORN AND FERGUSON ACQUIRE A SUPPLY NETWORK

A Dearborn Lift-Type Spring-Shank Cultivator made working a field with stones or roots less of a problem. The rolling coulter caused the cultivator to accurately track the tractor's steering in row crops. The cultivator weighs 356 pounds.

While not quite as important as the plow, the cultivator is still an important farm implement. That's why two types of cultivators were among the original tools Ferguson designed and fabricated for the Ferguson-Brown tractor.

Rigid shank and spring shank cultivators are generally used for row-crop cultivation, while Ferguson tiller and Dearborn field cultivators are designed for working in open fields.

A cultivator generally isn't considered an engineering coup from the design standpoint. However, the one difference that made the Ferguson design a novelty was its being rear-mounted on the three-point hitch. Without the draft control, it was mostly unsatisfactory, lacking a method of controlling the depth of the ground-engaging tines or shovels.

Ford engineer Harold Brock had this to say about the development of the cultivator at the Ford plant:

We did produce the cultivator as well. We had the same situation there with Ferguson. We designed the cultivator, then he said you had to set the shanks on a surface plate to make sure they all were exactly the same length and set exactly the same. This was kind of unusual, but we did it.

It (the Ferguson tractor) had steel wheels on it. And when we put the cultiva-

While using his Dearborn Lift-Type Spring-Shank Cultivator, the operator drives by steering according to an adjustable guide or "pointer" he has installed on his tractor's front axle using the regular bolt holes. This relieves operator tension, because the guide makes driving correctly down the rows so much easier.

tor that we designed on the little 9N tractor with rubber tires, whenever the hydraulic system called for a signal to raise it or lower it, it would overcompensate. The rubber tires would compress when the signal came and the hydraulics started to lift. Then the governor would take over and try to rev up to get more power, and then the cultivator would porpoise up and down.

We had to try it out in different soils, from sandy to clay, to try to change the hydraulics, for the hydraulic system he brought with him wasn't very satisfactory. We had to work on that confounded thing to make it work. We finally got it worked out to where it wouldn't porpoise, by changing the hydraulic control.

But even at this point, the rear-mounted row-crop units posed a major marketing challenge. For generations farmers had used cultivators that placed the tines or shovels ahead of the operator so the farmer had a clear view of the relationship of the tool to the row crop.

Marketing, therefore, required a generous amount of salesmanship and field demonstrations to convince farmers that the trailing cultivators would follow the tractor if the tractor was guided carefully. Complementary advertising material made the claim that the cultivator would follow the tractor "like a shadow."

Checking on The Shadow

Few farmers could resist the desire to check on "the shadow," however. This usually resulted in a sore neck and a wandering tractor path that destroyed crops. A guide to be mounted on the tractor's front axle was designed later, and it greatly aided precisely steering down the rows while cultivating.

Ferguson and his staff were eventually able to convince their distributors and dealerships

A Dearborn Rigid Shank Cultivator also utilizes a steering "fin" that keeps the implement stabilized and accurately following the tractor's track.

that the trailing, rear-mounted cultivator was a major step in a new concept of farming and was also marketable. The resistance was kind of a blessing in disguise at the time, though, because it allowed more development time for units headed onto the U.S. market. Ferguson's engineers again experienced difficulty grasping the difference between what would work in England's soils and in English manufacturing, and what would work in U.S. soils and suit U.S. manufacturing methods.

Willie Sands and Archie Greer were responsible for the English design that was produced before 1938. However, these models proved of little use as models for U.S. production. In late 1938, Ford engineers designed a cultivator that Ferguson immediately rejected. During this period he was focusing his time and that of his engineers on getting a tractor and plow in production. He had scheduled his "Invitation to the Land" demonstration for June 1939, and a tractor and implements had to be present for the demonstration to be successful.

Certain Ford and Ferguson engineers were given a mandate for a new cultivator design, and they produced a unit utilizing the standard Ferguson frame of two parallel angle irons drilled for shank attachment. Ford designed and cast one-piece tines that were "fixed" to the angle iron with

no adjustment capabilities. Although demonstration samples were produced, the design was scrubbed shortly thereafter. At this point, the cultivator project was contracted to the Empire Plow Company of Cleveland, Ohio, under the supervision of a Ferguson engineer, Dan McCullough.

This collaboration produced the KO rigid tine cultivator in the fall of 1939. Tests exposed several shortcomings, mainly insufficient clearance for trash to easily move through the tines and inadequate height clearance for crops. Redesigned with additional input from Ferguson engineers, the problems were solved. The shank placement was arranged further to the rear, and the shanks were fitted so a 3- to 4-inch height adjustment was possible. The redesigned unit was designated as the NKO rigid shank cultivator.

Empire began supplying Ferguson with cultivators in late 1939 or early 1940. In reality, Empire was more of a final assembler than a true manufacturer. As with the other implements, Ferguson contracted manufacture of the separate parts that were shipped to one final manufacturer for assembly before being sent on to Ferguson distributors. Empire manufactured the cultivator frames and did final assembly. The shanks, shovels, and other fixtures were produced by Pittsburgh Forgings or Tractor Appliance Company.

Don Horner, longtime Ford-Ferguson dealer, remembers that the cultivators were shipped semi-assembled. In 1940, he paid a man 50 cents to assemble each cultivator.

Ford Maintains a Prominent Role

The cultivator development seemed to be going nicely until a Ford Motor Company departmental communication dated October 4, 1939, appeared in regard to DO-7802 middlebuster beams. The memo said this piece was to be manufactured completely by Ford Motor Company, and sold to the Ferguson Sherman Company for delivery to B. F. Avery Company, Louisville, Kentucky. It directed the department to design and order equipment necessary to produce up to 1,200 a month. A second correspondence, dated December 7, 1939, addressed both middlebuster components and cultivator components:

The following are to be made by Ford Motor Company and sold to Ferguson-Sherman Manufacturing Corporation:
    KO 7825 Bracket-Cultivator Angle Front
    Mr. Reinhold: Furnish patterns
    Mr. Bullock: Schedule 1,200 pieces for December
    Mr. Pioch: Design and order necessary tools
    KO 7826 Bracket
    Mr. Bullock: Schedule 1,200 pieces for December. This is the same as used on KO and BO Cultivators.

An accompanying handwritten note said: "Mr. Murphy called and wanted to know if any decision had been reached regarding castings for cultivator parts, which castings are manufactured by Ford Motor Company, billed to F-S and shipped to Empire Plow, Cleveland, Ohio . . . two shipments have been made."

It's clear that Ford continued playing a major cooperative role during the initial development of the cultivator. In view of the fact that tooling was designed and purchased, it can be assumed this tooling was used in production of the cultivator part for some time. In this light, it may be easier to understand Ford's position on

This seven-shank tiller is an early Ferguson Type 9-BO-20 model. Later tillers mounted nine shanks. Each shank is attached to two large springs. This lets a shovel hit an obstacle in the ground, spring back, then move into working position without damage. This tiller is often used in orchards.

implements when the break took place between Ford and Ferguson.

In 1947, Dearborn desperately needed implements. For cultivators, Ford looked to the Pittsburgh Forgings Company, which had no farm implement experience other than the Ferguson account. Pittsburgh Forging was unqualified to independently develop a cultivator for Dearborn. Pittsburgh, however, did bring in an outside consultant who had previously worked for Minneapolis-Moline, Ferguson, and in the machinery design department of Kaiser-Frazer.

Circumventing the existing Ferguson patents was a foremost concern in designing a cultivator for Dearborn. It was also important to avoid similar appearances as much as possible. Dearborn replaced the Ferguson guide fin with a rolling coulter, which that wasn't yet available for the first distributor demonstrations. They increased the space between the two angle iron frame members by 1 inch—to 16 inches apart—and added extra bracing. It was critical that a cultivator unit be available for demonstrations. But new tooling for casting the Dearborn 16-inch shanks to fit the 16-inch spacing on the angle iron frame wasn't finished in time. So it's reported that Ferguson 15-inch shanks were cut and a 1-inch piece was welded in and ground smooth.

Once again the transition from Ferguson to Dearborn implements was a strange metamorphosis that incorporated something from both lines. The fact that the Ford people were concerned that Ferguson would raise allegations about Pittsburgh using his tooling to produce the parts for Dearborn implements probably justified any suspicions Ferguson had. Yet Ferguson never probed the issue. The reality is probably that both parties knew what was being done, but bigger issues overshadowed the cultivator issue. The thinking seems to have been: "Best let that sleeping dog lie."

Dearborn Prefers In-House Manufacturing

Dearborn didn't believe that the Ferguson system of diverse manufacturing was a good one. In contrast, Dearborn's staff believed that it was more cost-effective if a single manufacturer was responsible for the complete implement, or at least as much as was within its manufacturing

A spring-shank cultivator with 11 shanks enables the implement to work more effectively in soils with stones or roots. It's a Type SKO.

capacity. That's why Dearborn approached Pittsburgh, asking if it would, or could, manufacture the complete cultivator. The response was affirmative.

The first complete Pittsburgh cultivators were delivered to Dearborn in August 1947, when Pittsburgh shipped 881 rigid shank and spring shank cultivators. Once under way, production increased rapidly. By September, the monthly delivery volume was approximately 3,300 cultivators, and October production totaled approximately 5,700 units. Once Pittsburgh's new production facilities came on line, production rose to a reported 10,000 cultivators in March 1948. Delivery included some of all three models—rigid shank, spring shank, and field cultivators.

As production for Dearborn was accelerating, Ferguson stopped taking delivery of cultivator parts from Pittsburgh, and he instructed the company to stop all production of Ferguson parts. The inventory on hand had an estimated value of between $150,000 and $250,000.

By June 1948, Ferguson had satisfied his obligation for the stock inventory and continued to ship small numbers of the castings to Empire for cultivator assembly. Ferguson advised Pittsburgh that he would continue to do business with the firm as long as it was economically feasible. Pittsburgh had the manufacturing capacity to supply both Dearborn and Ferguson.

Towner Manufacturing Company in Santa Ana, California, had been in the implement business since just after the turn of the century. The company enjoyed an excellent reputation for manufacturing West Coast implements, which were usually considered a special line, although they varied little in appearance from other implements. The chief difference was the rugged nature of construction, because West Coast farming subjected the tools to much more wear than did farming in other parts of the country. Due to the climate and use of irrigation, farmers could regularly plant and harvest three or four crops per year. Thus, tools designed for one annual crop had approximately one-fourth the life expectancy when used on the West Coast and also in some southern states. Towner manufactured approximately 50 different implements or attachments, and the com-

pany had its own marketing organization. During wartime periods of material allotments, it had no difficulty selling everything it produced.

When the Ford-Ferguson tractor appeared in 1939, Towner adapted many of its existing implements to the three-point hitch. A considerable number of these implements were covered by U.S. patents. Probably as early as 1940, the Towner line of tractor-mounted implements was sold through Ferguson distributors on the West Coast and in southwestern states. It wasn't until 1942 or 1943 that the Ferguson organization began to press for exclusive distribution rights of the Towner line.

Towner at first resisted any agreement with Ferguson, because of War Production Board (WPB) quotas and the fact that it was already selling all it could produce. Contact was maintained, though, and by 1945 or 1946 an exclusive deal with Ferguson was being considered. There were several reasons Ferguson management pushed so hard for a formal agreement. It not only wanted an exclusive on sales, but also licensing rights to Tower's implement patents.

Towner Agrees to Terms

Concerning the state of implement design in 1948, Merritt Hill recalled, "After dealings between the two companies got under way, Ferguson contributed little to implement design, and (I) feel that to the present date Towner implement designs are 99 percent Towner-developed."

One possible reason Towner finally agreed to terms was that Ferguson's aggressive distribution network covered much more of the market area than did Towner's in-house marketing department. The two parties signed an agreement April 17, 1945, the same day a licensing agreement was signed.

Note this quote from the agreement, *ARTICLE XI—Products Design, Material and Workmanship*:

"Any product manufactured by Towner for distribution by Ferguson shall be produced in accordance with blueprints and specifications and under standard inspection requirements approved in writing by the Engineering Department of Ferguson. Towner shall make no change whatsoever in any approved construction, specification, or inspection requirement without first obtaining the written consent and approval of Ferguson."

It was a toss-up whether a dealer sold more plows or more 11-shank rigid Ferguson Type NKO cultivators like this one. Both were at the top of the list for three-point equipment popularity. The shanks can be spaced in 2-inch spacings throughout so row spacings can be altered to fit the crop conditions. The shanks are also adjustable for angle and height.

There are no records indicating Ferguson did, or didn't, produce such blueprints and specifications, but most likely he did.

Cultivators were definitely part of the Towner line. But for some reason, purchase records don't indicate that they were purchased by Ferguson, although they most surely were. Worksheets dated May 1947 show that Ferguson had the following on order with Towner for delivery between July and December:

Offset disc harrow
2,400
Spring-tooth harrow
5,850
Land leveler
600
Trip dump scraper
1,200
Buck scraper
1,500
Attachments
6,000

Cultivator order numbers apparently were few, if Dearborn's first purchase agreement is any indication. For March and April 1948, only 310 spring-tooth cultivators were ordered. In contrast, nearly 1,000 offset discs were ordered.

Just how Dearborn became a Towner customer highlights the "implement drama" that surrounded the handshake agreement's demise. It also emphasizes again the importance of both a tractor source and an implement source for successfully marketing the mounted implement system.

Hill resigned from Ferguson on July 31, 1946, after being on the West Coast as Ferguson's regional manager since earlier that year. He organized the Western Implement Merchandisers, Inc., and soon obtained the distribution of the Towner general line of implements in all West Coast and southwestern states except California and Arizona, where Towner maintained sales staffs. The general line didn't include the three-point implements. It seems that Hill was playing on both sides of the fence by keeping constant contact with Ferguson and other major implement distributors and dealers in the territory.

Ferguson Tries to Develop Own Tractor

It had become common knowledge that Ferguson was trying to develop a new tractor source. Rumors were flying like ducks in autumn. One such rumor, quoted in a dealer letter, even said that Ferguson was on the lam from the FBI. Industry management, no doubt including Towner, believed that a break between Ford and Ferguson was imminent. Dearborn's first contact with Towner management probably was made by Hill in May or June. That's when he called Towner to explore the possibility of working out an arrangement between Towner and Dearborn.

By this time, Dearborn was holding meetings to inform, and if possible, sign up distributors and dealers on the West Coast. Ferguson had the implements, but no tractor. Now Dearborn had a tractor to sell but was virtually without implements to accompany the tractors. It's no surprise that dealers' most often-asked question was, "When can we have the Towner line of implements?"

Hill had negotiated the original Towner agreement with Ferguson, so he was aware it

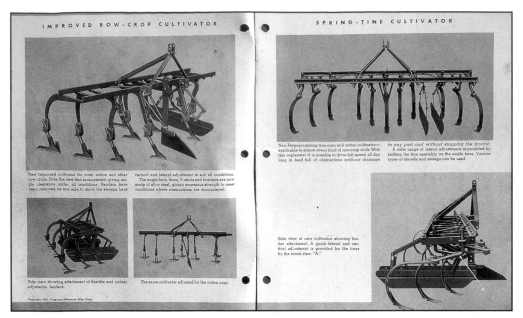

IMPROVED ROW-CROP CULTIVATOR

New improved cultivator for corn, cotton and other row crops. Note the new tine arrangement giving ample clearance under all conditions. Fenders have been removed on one side to show the sweeps have vertical and lateral adjustment to suit all conditions. The angle bars, tines, V-struts and brackets are now made of alloy steel, giving enormous strength to meet conditions where obstructions are encountered.

Side view showing attachment of flexible and widely adjustable fenders.

The same cultivator adjusted for the cotton crop.

Copyright 1941, Ferguson-Sherman Mfg. Corp.

SPRING-TINE CULTIVATOR

New Ferguson spring-tine corn and cotton cultivator—applicable to almost every kind of row-crop work. With this implement it is possible to drive full speed all day long in land full of obstructions *without damage* to any part and without stopping the tractor. A wide range of lateral adjustments is provided by shifting the tine assembly on the angle bars. Various types of shovels and sweeps can be used.

Side view of new cultivator showing fender attachment. A quick lateral and vertical adjustment is provided for the tines by the crank stem "A."

This specification sheet is from 1941 Ferguson-Sherman Manufacturing Company product literature on cultivators.

This graphic plus description in a Ferguson manual explains the purpose of the "fin" and how it helps "steer" the cultivator.

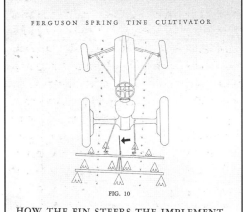

FERGUSON SPRING TINE CULTIVATOR

FIG. 10

HOW THE FIN STEERS THE IMPLEMENT

If, for example, the operator allows the tractor to get too close to the crop as shown at the left rear wheel, he then steers the tractor central again as shown by the front wheels.

The instant the front wheels are turned to steer the tractor back to the center of the row, a heavy soil pressure is imposed all along the side of the fin, as indicated by the arrow. This causes the fin to deflect and steer the implement *to follow the front wheels*, as shown.

On hillsides the tendency of the implement to fall away puts a soil pressure along the side of the fin. This steers the implement up the hill and keeps it in the correct position.

Best crops can only be obtained by perfect cultivation and perfect cultivation is impossible unless it be done at the rear, as perfected in the Ferguson System. The fin can justly be called a revolutionary invention because rear end cultivation would be impossible without it.

9

contained a one-year notice-of-termination clause. Other West Coast manufacturers were approached and evaluated, too. Still, Hill decided it would be better to wait on the Towner line with its greater sales potential.

When Hill first contacted Towner, he was advised by Towner management that they had always enjoyed a most satisfactory relationship with Ferguson. They also pointed out they had a contract that prohibited sales to Dearborn. Towner was sticking with Ferguson even though Ferguson sales were shrinking at an alarming rate. At this point, near-desperation in the Dearborn camp produced a most-novel strategic move by the West Coast dealers and distributors. Even though they knew Towner couldn't honor them, they decided to send purchase orders directly to Towner so Towner management could see just how much business it was missing by staying with Ferguson.

The orders that rolled in and piled up at Towner produced the desired result. Towner contacted Ferguson to explore the possibility of renegotiating their contract, or of canceling the contract completely and accepting the consequences. However, further negotiation provided a solution that was acceptable, if not ideal, to all parties. Ferguson granted Towner a release from the contract provision preventing Towner of selling to Dearborn. Dearborn would have preferred an exclusive arrangement, but gladly accepted the terms and the implements.

Ferguson was able to stipulate that his orders for production were to receive priority in Towner plants. The renegotiation was finalized in September 1947.

Early in February 1948, Towner opened a new plant at Stockton, California, for production of its general line. With this added manufacturing capacity, it had no difficulty producing enough implements for both the Ferguson and Dearborn needs.

The years 1946 and 1947 were extremely trying for both organizations. Longtime employees, distributors, and dealers of Harry Ferguson, Inc., had to make a choice. Should they stay with the man and the organization that had brought the system so far along the road to success? Or should they hedge their bets and join Dearborn, which was obviously backed by the preponderant wealth and prestige of the Ford Motor Company? A majority chose the latter.

At this point, Harry Ferguson was badly battered and bruised, but by no means was he out of the fight. Just how much time Ferguson spent in the United States during this time is difficult to determine. Indications are that he relied almost exclusively on the management at his Dearborn, Michigan, offices. In a letter from Ireland, Ferguson agreed, "It is difficult to start over." But, with typical Ferguson tenacity, he did so and rebounded to where his Ferguson tractors and implements were again selling well.

Middlebusters

The middlebuster was one of the original three-point implements to accompany the Ferguson-Brown tractor. Even though it served quite a specialized farming application, it was one of the early implements to be offered with the N-Series tractors.

As far as can be established, the plow was the only complete implement manufactured at the Ford plant. There's also ample evidence that Ford manufactured subassemblies for some other implements. An October 4, 1939, departmental document indicates Ford was producing middlebuster beams "To be manufactured completely by Ford Motor Company" and delivered to B. F. Avery Company of Louisville, Kentucky.

Ford was to design and purchase tooling in order to produce 1,200 units a month. This suggests that the middlebuster was either already in production or would be shortly, and that the implement was destined to be part of the line for some time.

It's easy to confuse the middlebuster and the ridger, because they have visual and functional similarities. Both utilize a frame similar in design to the cultivator frames with two parallel angle irons, to which the bottoms are attached. The frame of the middlebuster isn't as wide as the cultivator frame, though it has two large two-way bases attached, each able to open a furrow 12 to 14 inches wide.

The ridger is fitted with three bases, each a small two-way plow base much smaller than that used by the middlebuster. In either instance, the base design was developed long before the three-point implements were established.

The stabilizing "fin" is vital to proper operation of the Ferguson cultivators, because it reacts to steering wheel inputs of the operator to keep the cultivator properly positioned.

As with the plow bases, a standard base from an old-line supplier was adapted to fit the Ferguson frame. Cockshutt Plow Company of Canada supplied some of these ridger bases.

For middlebuster bases, Ferguson contracted at various times with David Bradley Manufacturing Company, B. F. Avery Company, and the Kelly Plow Company. The Empire Plow Company served as an assembler of several types of Ferguson implements, including the middlebuster. It looks like Empire came on line in or around 1943. It's not known if the number of middlebusters assembled and shipped that year was in addition to Ford's beam production or a part of it.

Empire had the capabilities and capacity to produce the frames and did so for cultivators and ridgers. In the first six months of 1946, Ferguson bought approximately 950 middlebusters from Empire.

Whether or not it was standard practice then, it's interesting that the agreement with Empire for assembly was based on the weight of the components assembled; Empire was paid a certain amount per hundred pounds of weight.

Harry Ferguson, Inc., President Roger Kyes began an implement procurement cutback in the summer of 1946 that reduced orders as much as 80 percent on many implements. This was at the time Ford had made the decision to stop tractor shipment to Ferguson on or before the end of 1946. Whether Harry Ferguson was in the United States during the crisis is unclear. Most of the evidence suggests he wasn't. Apparently he had complete faith in Kyes to handle the situation. This faith seems to have been well-placed, because in November 1946, a Ford-Ferguson interim tractor agreement was executed that would supply Ferguson with approximately 50,000 additional tractors to be delivered through June 1947.

With that document in hand, Kyes reinstated many of the implement orders, such as those for 1947 delivery from Empire of 22,080 cultivators and tillers; 4,200 middlebuster frames; and 1,200 ridgers.

Dearborn's Role Expands

Just months after this interim agreement was executed, Kyes proposed that Dearborn assume all of Ferguson's implement commitments. A conference was held between the two parties in the spring of 1947. Of course, Dearborn management also hoped it could step in and pick up the supplier and distribution networks intact, as this November 1, 1946, Dearborn memo notes:

This entire study (sales projections) has been made with the thought in mind that we would continue the distribution program as it presently functions under the Ferguson organization, using their same distributor and dealer setup. It is, likewise, predicated upon the premise that Ferguson's present suppliers would supply us with the implements as outlined in our Schedule of Estimated Sales . . .

For whatever reasons, an agreement between Ferguson and Dearborn was never actually signed. Dearborn probably took a hard bargaining position based on the odds that Ferguson would cease to exist after June 1947, and Dearborn rejected the Ferguson proposal. Shortly after the meeting, Kyes canceled most outstanding orders with Empire Plow Company.

Ferguson still had a contract with Empire, however, and there was strong loyalty between the two companies. Empire wasn't considered as a manufacturer by Dearborn for a number of reasons: Dearborn's interest was in a front-mounted cultivator to replace the rear-mounted one Empire was providing, Dearborn wasn't going to offer a ridger, and the middlebuster was low in priority.

The G. A. Kelly Plow Company of Longview, Texas, entered the picture as a Ferguson supplier in 1941 or 1942. This relationship's development is interesting because it illustrates how more than one implement found its way into the three-point implement line. Kelly was an old company, dating back to 1850 or thereabouts, and its entire line was designed for specialty farming in southern and southwestern states.

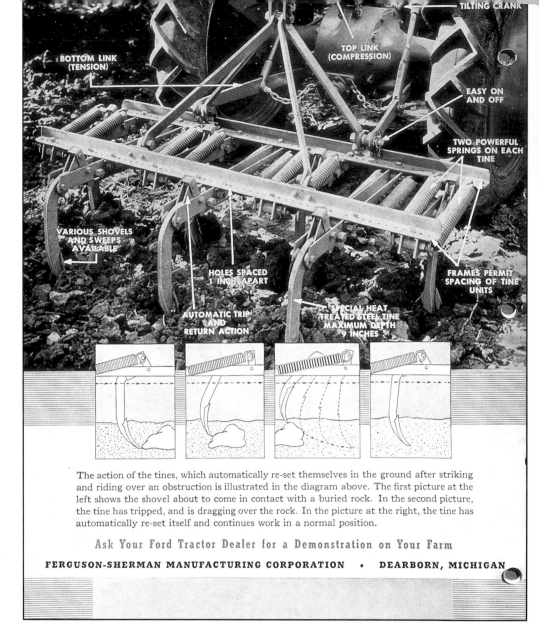

The action of the tines, which automatically re-set themselves in the ground after striking and riding over an obstruction is illustrated in the diagram above. The first picture at the left shows the shovel about to come in contact with a buried rock. In the second picture, the tine has tripped, and is dragging over the rock. In the picture at the right, the tine has automatically re-set itself and continues work in a normal position.

Ask Your Ford Tractor Dealer for a Demonstration on Your Farm

FERGUSON-SHERMAN MANUFACTURING CORPORATION • DEARBORN, MICHIGAN

This leaflet does an outstanding job of both showing the implement and explaining how one of its most important features works. It also advises the reader to ask for a demonstration on his own farm.

Dearborn's first appraisal of the Kelly plant in November 1947 described the facility like this:

This plant is small and most of the equipment is rather old. They have their own small gray iron foundry, a forging shop, and their own lumber yard in addition to the necessary equipment for drilling holes and machining.

This plant appeared to have been changed little in the past 30 years. They

Made in England, this Ferguson three-point implement mounts three blades, so it's a ridger and not a middlebuster.

This is a pre-1943 Ferguson-Sherman row-crop cultivator.

Ferguson-Sherman manufactured this tiller sometime before 1943.

make a line of one- and two-horse plows, listers, cultivators, planters, and a few spike-tooth harrows and disc harrows. Many of these items are comparatively low volume.

Mr. Marvin Kelly, son of the founder, is still active in the management of the plant despite the fact that he is 86 years old.

During the past year or so they have lost some of their older management personnel and the purchasing, production, and experimental work are under three young men in their early thirties. I do not believe that they have any Engineering Department, and I would take it that the shop works from patterns rather than from drawings.

Kelly Sees N-Series Opportunities

Kelly, in common with many other small manufacturers, saw the introduction of the N-Series tractor as a great opportunity. Through simple modification of its existing product it could provide a mounted model for farmers who were looking for additional implements to fit their new tractors. Soon after the 9N was introduced in 1939, it appears that Kelly sold planter attachments for use on the Ferguson cultivator frame to Bull-Stewart, a Dallas, Texas, distributor of the Ford-Ferguson. It's probable that Kelly also sold these attachments to several other southwestern distributors.

At that time Kelly had its own horse-drawn line of middlebusters. Whether it adapted these bases to the Ferguson cultivator frame isn't altogether clear. A good guess would be that it did, because Avery (Ferguson's middlebuster supplier at the time) wasn't able to provide Ferguson the production it needed to meet demand.

Although Ferguson's primary interest was in Kelly's planter units, having a ready supply of middlebusters would be an added bonus. Kelly also had other three-point implements in the developmental stage. Even though the Kelly plant was somewhat outdated, its affiliation with Ferguson was pursued vigorously by the Ferguson procurement staff.

During the first six months, 954 middlebusters were manufactured. In the same period a year later, purchases and delivery had risen to 3,635 units. It's not certain if Kelly manufactured the entire middlebuster or if it obtained components from other manufacturers. Either way, it does seem that Kelly had difficulties meeting Ferguson's demands for implements. Hill remembers that by 1946 Kelly always fell far short of Ferguson requirements. It's thought that Kelly was excluded from the purchasing cutback in the summer of 1946. There's also some indication that during the mid-1940s, Kelly had expanded its production facilities.

Records of the Kyes and Dearborn meeting in the spring of 1947, in which Kyes proposed that Dearborn assume Ferguson's implement commitments, show that Ferguson had orders for 9,000 middlebuster bases. This would indicate that Kelly was tooled up to produce bases. Because they're listed separately from completed units, it follows that Kelly was supplying bases to another firm for assembly. This was probably Empire Plow Company or B. F. Avery.

Dearborn's procurement department was especially interested in Kelly's planters first, and in the middlebusters only as a secondary product. Actually, Pittsburgh Forging was Dearborn's middlebuster supplier of frames and final assembly. It didn't have a source for bases, though. Kelly was the base supplier, although it was never able to produce adequate numbers.

Once the Dearborn organization had a better handle on volume requirements for middlebusters, it revised its projected numbers downward. As of 1948, Pittsburgh Forging and Kelly were the only middlebuster suppliers.

Two power springs on each tine allow this seven-tine tiller to be operated in rocky ground with little damage.

Called a middlebuster, this piece of Ferguson equipment has one large V-blade. It was generally used in the fall to ridge fields in an attempt to help trap as much winter snow and rain as possible. The implement could also be used to make a furrow in which garden crops could be planted. It is a Type DO-21.

A Ferguson cultivator moves over a field two rows at a time. It's mounted on a tractor that has had its wheels moved out.

This nine-tine rigid Ferguson tiller was made in England.

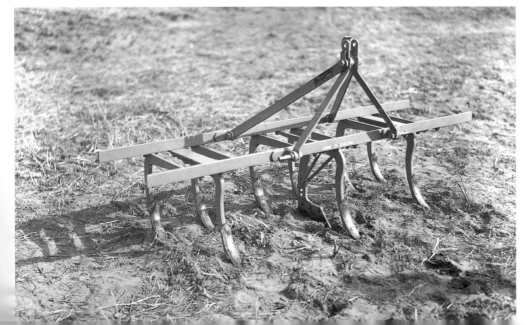

CHAPTER SEVEN

Mowers and Rakes

AN EXHAUSTIVE SEARCH YIELDS THE RIGHT MOWER

A sturdy, side-mounted Ferguson mower is attached to a 9N tractor. Its identification

plate shows it to be a Type 56 PE-O21.

t's likely any engineer would agree that mowers were one of the more difficult implements to design among all the three-point implements available for the N-Series tractors. Farmers would agree that mowers are critical to many farming operations, a view recognized by Henry Ford, and probably by Harry Ferguson as well, from the early days of their agreement. Howard Simpson, Ford's original 9N engineer, resigned from Ford in 1939 to join Detroit Harvester Company as its chief engineer. His written records regarding mower development pointed out:

About August 1939, Ford requested designs of mowing machines for the new tractor from the Detroit Harvester Company, and I conferred with Ferguson and Sherman at the Rouge plant about this. We designed and built up an experimental mower and delivered it October 30, 1939. This mower was apparently satisfactory but had many details to be improved. On December 31, we delivered an improved model.

A bit of information contained in each implement file pursuant to the lawsuit gave an estimate of an engineering developmental cycle for that particular implement. For mowers, including fundamental designing and field testing, the estimate given was that it would normally require two or three years.

The Dyna-Balance Ferguson mower carries this easily seen plate. It sums up important lubrication information by not only noting when the mower needs greasing, but also by detailing the zerk fittings involved so none are missed.

Detroit Harvester delivered a mower in two to three months by using the industry's standard practice, which could almost be called a credo, "never design what you can modify."

Detroit Harvester began in 1922 as a farm implement manufacturer, and by the 1930s had entered into auto accessories and parts manufacturing, which became the most prominent division of the company. Ford Motor Company was one of Harvester's accounts. So it isn't surprising that its name would come up as a supplier for parts for the Ford-Ferguson project. The first product, or attachment, Harvester made for the 9N was the power takeoff. It was supplied to Ford, which in turn sold it to Ferguson. However, Harvester may have been a reluctant supplier. H. L. Pierson, president of

Harvester, reportedly was ready to give testimony that the only reason Harvester did business with Ferguson was because of Ford.

But, it did do business. Mowers were in demand. The experimental mower in all likelihood was an adaptation of the side-mower previously developed by Harvester for the J. J. Case tractor.

Mower has Room for Improvement

With Ferguson engineering personnel stretched thin due to demands for implement design, it's probable that the design modifications were made by Harvester personnel. However, Ferguson would have had final say in design approval, of course. Simpson records show the experimental model had such excessive vibration that it damaged the tractor's housing. Installing a heavier flywheel and counterweights on the flywheel helped reduce the vibration. But the mower was still unfit to be a production model. In March 1940, Sorensen suggested that a tubular frame be constructed to encircle the tractor and the mower attached to that. Simpson's notes for April 2, 1940, indicated:

We finally got what we thought Ford accepted as a complete design on the mower and we built about 10 mowers up and sent them out to the Rouge plant. I think we built about 100 with this tubular frame that Mr. Sorensen had suggested. It never was a satisfactory design. In the first

The rear-mounted Dearborn mower represents a slight advancement over the previous mowers available for the N-Series tractors. Once in place, it worked quite well. However, the attempt by one person to attach it can be both frustrating and a time-eater. The task goes much faster with two people, and even more rapidly with three people.

in the mower works, and because WPB price restrictions prevented Harvester from passing the increasing production costs on to Ferguson.

Naturally, this placed mowers in a low priority for production. To get more production out the door, Kyes authorized a payment of $50,000 to help pay some of Harvester's operating losses.

Adding the Rear-Mount to the Line

The Ferguson-Sherman implement line included the side-mount mower as early as 1940. A rear-mount mower didn't join the line until 1942 or 1943. Certainly the demand for mowers was sufficient to justify adding a rear-mount at the same time as the side-mount. There's evidence that Harvester continued on its own to design and develop a rear-mounted unit. Just why this mower didn't find its way into the Ferguson line until probably 1944 is an interesting story. Of course, conclusions drawn 50-plus years later are mostly speculative. But some compelling evidence is found in a May 22, 1948, "Memorandum of fact," in the *Ferguson vs. Ford* files:

Sometime during the spring of 1944, Hill (Ferguson procurement) asked Pierson (Harvester president) whether Harvester would cooperate in the developmental work on the new Ferguson rear mower and produce it when design and specifications were completed. Pierson replied that Harvester had already completed a new design of mower specifically for use with the 9N tractor.

In fact, Harvester had designed a mower attachable to the 9N tractor linkage some two or three years earlier, and it had been displayed to various people in the Ferguson organization. Ferguson had regularly rejected the Harvester design (mainly due to professional pride on the part of Ferguson engineers, according to Hill) and had proceeded with its rear mower development project.

Is it possible that the Ferguson organization, specifically the engineering department, would waste two or three years getting a product into the line strictly because of pride?

place it was very clumsy. It had about three-inch tubing surrounding this tractor, and the tubing had to be bent to follow the contour of the tractor.

We went along with Sorensen on that and built about 100 of those. In the meantime, we designed a different mower. Instead of building a long frame, we built the frame just the length of a transmission housing and bolted it at the front and rear end of the transmission so that we could mount the mower on that.

This proved very satisfactory and was so much cheaper and easier to assemble. This became a standard mower and it is still a standard construction on the Ford tractor and Ferguson tractor also. I designed that

while I was chief engineer at Detroit Harvester Company. My diary ends on December 12, 1940, and I note that 250 mowers were nearing completion at that time with 171 shipped to date.

In 1941, Merritt Hill took charge of Ferguson's purchasing program. This was probably either when Kyes came on board or after Sherman and Ferguson got into conflict over implements. In an effort to increase mower production, a Ferguson representative was placed full-time at the Harvester plant. He was there to expedite production of mowers around the war work to which Harvester was committed.

Harvester was losing money on every mower it made because of a manpower shortage

Here's a close-up view of the side-mount Ferguson mower that shows some of its controls and also how the sickle was secured into the transport position.

Of course, the war restrictions on material and war work priorities were causing havoc with production facilities all across the country. Harvester in particular was experiencing this dilemma. Also, remember that Kyes issued a $50,000 check to Harvester when side-mount mower production was languishing at Harvester. It's possible that Ferguson management didn't want a repeat of the first mower episode, which could be viewed as a $50,000 blackmail.

In view of what happened to rear-mount mower design and development during 1940 to 1943, there must have been strong reasons that Harvester wasn't considered at the time. There are few reasons stronger than pride and money. Whatever the reasons, Ferguson in 1941 approached David Bradley Manufacturing Company for a rear-mount mower. Bradley was a division of Sears, Roebuck & Co. and was already a supplier of plowshares and bases to Ferguson. Bradley had developed a rear-mounted mower for other tractor makes that farmers were buying and modifying to fit the 9N. The mower wasn't efficient, and depending on the conversion, could be extremely difficult to mount. Nevertheless, Ferguson's procurement staff decided that the quickest solution to the need for a rear-mounted mower would be to adapt the Bradley design.

Teaming Up to Design a Mower

Probably during 1942, the Ferguson and Bradley engineering departments redesigned the Bradley mower to fit the 9N. Bradley agreed to furnish the redesigned unit to Ferguson as the "Ferguson Mower." Both sides considered this a temporary measure since the design was far from perfect. In fact, it was just barely acceptable. A better design was needed for a permanent solution to the rear-mount mower needs.

From Ferguson's standpoint, the problem with the Bradley mower wasn't just in its mechanical design. It doesn't appear that there was any written agreement to cover production numbers or priorities. And Ferguson definitely didn't have an exclusive on the mower. Ferguson found that Bradley was marketing the same, identical mower through Sears at a retail price below dealer cost in

This is the rear view of the side-mount Ferguson mower. It, too, can be a very difficult to attach. Two or, better yet, three people make the job go much more pleasantly and with fewer scarred knuckles.

some cases. All indications are that Bradley could have sold its entire production of mowers through Sears if it had so chosen.

As was the case in many other factories, Bradley's war work often interfered with mower production. The bottom line is that Ferguson soon came to consider Bradley an unsatisfactory vendor for mowers. Ferguson requested, and finally received, permission in 1944 from Bradley to seek another supplier for the Bradley-designed mower. Ferguson chose the firm of Central Architectural Iron Works, which established a division for implement manufacture called Farm Rite.

The parent company had a strong history of steel fabrication, but had never produced farm implements. Ferguson gave considerable assistance in negotiating with suppliers for raw materials and subassemblies. Also, the Ferguson staff persuaded Bradley's production superintendent to leave Bradley and join Farm Rite. This new vendor proved a capable supplier, and it soon took over all rear-mounted mower manufacturing. The original agreement between Bradley and Ferguson said the latter could have other suppliers only when Bradley couldn't satisfy order volumes, yet there's no indication Bradley ever complained about the loss of mower business. A bigger problem for Ferguson was the mower design itself. In 1944, Ferguson engineers started designing a new mower for three-point attachment to the 9N tractor.

Some pressure was brought by the Ferguson group to approach Harvester and cooperate with the company on the new mower design. Apparently Ferguson engineers were having difficulty finding either the right design or the time to address new mower needs. So, in late 1944, they gave some consideration to the Harvester design. Field tests between the Ferguson mower and Harvester showed superior performance by the Harvester implement.

It's likely that during 1945 Harvester began to produce rear-mounted mowers for Ferguson. At the same time the Bradley design was also being supplied by Farm Rite. In late 1945, Farm Rite was dropped as a mower supplier.

Harvester Increases Production Capacity

Harvester expanded its production facilities by purchasing a plant at Zanesville, Ohio, and moved all its mower production to this location. It's believed that from that date on, Harvester was Ferguson's sole supplier of mowers. From January to September 1946, Ferguson bought 4,543 rear-mount mowers and 8,122 side-mount mowers from Harvester.

During the 1946 implement order cutbacks by Ferguson, Hill didn't believe Ferguson could pare mower orders, because mowers were always in short supply. Records reveal that Ferguson purchase projections for 1947 amounted to 1,000 side-mount units a month and 3,000 rear-mount units a month. When the Dearborn procurement department began making projections for implement needs, it based them on estimated tractor production of 400 tractors a day. Its estimate for mowers for the last half of 1947 totaled 8,000 mowers.

There's little evidence that Dearborn seriously considered any other supplier than Harvester for its mowers. And changing vendors wasn't all that easy since it would have to wait a year before it could get out of the contract.

The side-mower didn't have the problems of the rear-mount unit, nor was the side-mower attached to the three-point system—in case Ferguson should claim novelty design for the three-point linkage. The redesign necessary to fit it to the 8N would make it exempt from the Ferguson-Harvester agreement on side-mount mowers.

Harvester already had a long-time business relationship with Ford. After considering the likelihood of a Ford-Ferguson split, it came down firmly on the Ford-Dearborn side and expressed a desire to supply mowers for the new company.

Another issue was especially critical concerning the rear-mount mowers. Dearborn knew Ferguson's strong suit, if it came to litigation, would be the three-point mounting system. If Harvester redesigned the mower to circumvent any similarity, then it might pose a sales problem to distributors and dealers who were concerned about whether the new Dearborn line of implements would fit the 9N and 2N tractors. More than 300,000 of these trac-

This Ferguson rear-mounted mower from the early 1940s features a 6-foot sicklebar that's lowered into working position. It never gained great popularity because it vibrated rather badly. Also, as the present owner reports with understatement, "It's also, well, call it difficult to mount."

tors were in the hands of farmers, and it would certainly hurt sales if the implements couldn't be interchanged between the tractors.

Ford engineers considered parallel linkage for the new 8N instead of the converging linkage of the Ford-Ferguson tractor. They thought this would be sufficient to avoid patent claims and still have a hitching system that would accommodate both the old and new implement designs. In fact, the first 8Ns shown to dealers had parallel linkage. When the decision was

made to use converging linkage on the new 8N tractor, engineering time and money were spent by Ford to change the attachment design of the new mower and offer a kit that would make the new mower usable with the 9N and 2N tractor. Later developments made this unnecessary.

Ferguson had been negotiating for financing and a facility in which to build his own tractor, hoping to make it available shortly after the supply from Ford stopped. Preliminary negotiations were under way to establish this plant in Cleveland,

This Dyna-Balance Ferguson mower carries a 7-foot sicklebar. What's unique about this mower is that it has what's described in sales literature as a balanced head. It reads Type F-EO-20 on its identification plate. This mower has a little crankshaft built into it. Although most mowers vibrate and shake abundantly, this model is virtually vibration-free. As its owner notes, "There doesn't seem to be any vibration whatsoever. And the mower just runs and runs and runs. Everybody who's owned one of these mowers just loves it."

Ohio. Ferguson was forced to cut back implement orders and give ground on his exclusive agreement with suppliers when the expected financing fell through. Little information was found to substantiate the exact nature of the agreement whereby Ferguson relaxed its exclusive agreement. However, it probably happened in June 1947, and it left Harvester able to supply both types of mowers to the Dearborn organization.

Differences Among Mowers

There was one notable difference between the Ferguson and Dearborn mowers. The Ferguson side-mower throws in the clutch of the tractor if the mower cutter bar encounters a solid obstruction. The Dearborn was designed to cut off the tractor ignition if the cutter bar struck such an object. The rear-mount mowers

Dearborn purchased from Harvester had two differences from the Ferguson models: color and the identification plate.

A note of interest to restorers can be found in an August 29, 1947, letter from Farm Rite to Harry Ferguson, Inc., concerning cancellation charges on the AEO mower service.

The letter lists charges incurred to Torrington Company for bearings, Jones & Laughlin Steel Corp. for shafting, and Sherwin Williams Co. for 855 one-gallon drums of gray paint for the AEO mower service and MKO weeder. Too bad that color specifications of gray weren't included.

Dearborn tried unsuccessfully to obtain an exclusive purchase agreement with Harvester, but Harvester rejected this proposal and continued to supply Ferguson and J. I. Case with mowers.

Rakes

Remember how Dearborn used its dealers as leverage to convince Towner to join the Dearborn bandwagon? Interestingly enough, the originality of this method could be credited to Ferguson dealers during negotiations with the Western Land Roller Company of Hastings, Nebraska.

In December 1942, Merritt Hill, in charge of Ferguson's procurement, contacted Western to discuss bringing the firm into the fold of Ferguson suppliers. Western had previously sold its implements—land rollers, feed grinders, sweep rakes, hay stackers, and pumps—through several Ferguson distributors that its own sales force had established. In some other instances they sold directly to Ferguson dealers.

Ferguson side-delivery rake looks even better than new. It was touted to "Move hay less distance from swatch to windrow."

Western employed a staff of seven salesmen and spent $35,000 annually on trade paper and direct mail advertising. Western was cautious about any arrangement with Ferguson—and, indirectly, Ford—because they, too, had been hurt when Ford withdrew the Fordson tractor from production in 1928. Western was definitely not interested in an exclusive arrangement. Since the company was curious, though, the president of Western wrote to the Ferguson dealers and distributors asking for their input. The letter-writing began in earnest as dealers replied to Western and, to a man, advised Western to join Ferguson. The letters reportedly carried a strong suggestion that if Western didn't go with Ferguson, another supplier would be found to replace the Western line they were now selling. Western signed up, figuratively anyway, granting Ferguson distribution rights for its implements. It's unclear whether there ever was a Ferguson-Western contract.

Western immediately shipped a sweep rake, also called a buck rake, to Ferguson in 1943 so Ferguson engineers could evaluate the unit. Ferguson apparently didn't suggest or recommend changes at this time, as the first Ferguson sweep rakes were essentially of Western design. The first sweep rake was supplied in 1944, when Ferguson took delivery of 960 during the first 6 months. Demand and production escalated during 1945. In the first 9 months of 1946, Ferguson bought more than 11,000 such sweep rakes, then the popularity of sweep rakes waned. Every indication is that Ferguson all but stopped placing any orders for this item from Western. At this time, Ferguson engineers had patented designs for a new sweep rake and also for a side delivery rake.

Little is known about the details of Western's change from Ferguson to Dearborn. The bottom line is that Dearborn ascertained that the sweep rake was the only implement Western sold to Ferguson, and Western was able and willing to sell to Dearborn. Dearborn then cut a purchase order in April 1947 for 5,000 sweep rakes to be delivered during the second half of the year. The consensus of involved parties was that the sweep rakes supplied to Ferguson and Dearborn were identical except for color.

There is also evidence that Dearborn had overestimated the demand for sweep rakes of the wooden tooth design. In the fall of 1947 Dearborn canceled 3,000 units of the 5,000-unit order. The wooden tooth design was being replaced with a metal tooth design, and even more importantly, the sweep rake was being replaced with more modern methods of haying. It's doubtful that Ferguson or Dearborn placed any additional orders for the Western sweep rake of wooden tooth design.

Here's an up-close and personal view of the Dyna-Balance Ferguson mower with 7-foot sicklebar. It doesn't have the usual pitman.

This is a similar side-delivery rake. However, even though it's well into its fifth decade since leaving the factory, it's still being used every summer to reliably move alfalfa into windrows.

CHAPTER EIGHT

Planters

DEMPSTER PRODUCTS FOR FERGUSON & DEARBORN

This two-row lister planter is Type DO-21. It was supplied as an attachment for the Ferguson middlebuster frame as a corn or cotton planter with press wheels. It's adjustable for row spacing. The planter is automatically thrown out of gear when it's raised by the fingertip hydraulic control. And while nobody called it "minimum tillage" back in the 1940s, with this two-row lister planter, a crop could be put in stubble fields in one pass.

Nothing indicates Ferguson had any type of planter or lister for the U.S. market in his implement line in 1939. Engineering estimates in the Henry Ford Archives place the time required to develop a properly designed and field-tested planter at between three to five years. So it's not surprising that an adaptation from an existing planter would be essential for demonstrations and initial sales.

Harold Brock was an employee of Ford Motor Company when the Ford-Ferguson agreement was struck, and was closely involved with the development of the project. Brock recalls that most of the emphasis was on the tractor. Once the tractor was essentially completed, though, they realized that they didn't have any satisfactory implements—and that the tractor wouldn't be worth much without implements to fit its three-point hitch.

He remembers that they purchased a disc harrow and were able to attach a three-point hitch to it without undue difficulty. However, the planter—an important tool for farmers—was a problem. One solution was the Covington horse-drawn planter on which they put a three-point hitch. They believed the tractor would replace many of the horses on farms, so farmers would already have horse-drawn planters they could adapt to the three-point system.

Ford didn't continue with planter production, either with conversions or direct manufac-

This late Ferguson two-row corn planter also carried fertilizer boxes. What's unusual about it is that these fertilizer boxes are still in pretty good condition, while most have rusted out almost completely by now.

ture. Perhaps, Brock said, Covington became a supplier for Ferguson. This was probably the beginning of the three-point planter.

Outside manufacturing firms immediately saw the opportunity to fit their planters to the three-point mounted system. In many cases they were able to address the problem before Ferguson or Ford could.

The G. A. Kelly Plow Company of Longview, Texas, adapted its horse-drawn planters to the three-point system shortly after introduction of the 9N. The development of the planters and fertilizer attachments closely paralleled the middlebuster, with which Kelly was already working. Kelly agreed to make certain minor design changes to its planters once Kelly and Ferguson had struck a deal. It was decided by Ferguson engineers that a complete new frame would be designed for the planters. They also con-

cluded that the planters should be sold complete with the frame instead of as a separate attachment for the cultivator frames.

The frame was redesigned, but the hole locations remained the same so Kelly attachments could be used with the planter frame. In addition to the frame, substantial improvements were made to the planting attachments by Ferguson engineers, but exactly what these changes were isn't specified. The best available information suggests that Ferguson began receiving planters from Kelly in 1941. During the negotiations with Kelly, Ferguson engineers were working on their own designs for corn and cotton planters. A 1944 memo shows that the project was still a way from completion, though. It was easy for Ferguson's purchasing department to decide to continue sourcing planters from both Kelly and Dempster Mill Manufacturing Company.

Dempster Made 9N Implements Early On

Dempster, like Kelly and others, had adapted its implements to the three-point system. Dempster, located in Beatrice, Nebraska, made these implements available shortly after the 9N appeared in dealership showrooms. Charles B. Dempster founded the company in 1878. He originally sold and installed pumps and windmills, which were manufactured by other companies in the East. In 1887, his company started production in its own facilities on

DRILL-TYPE TWO-ROW CORN PLANTER
for the new Ford tractor with Ferguson system

ACCURATE PLANTING MADE EASIER

● As in plowing, cultivating and other work, the Ford tractor with Ferguson system of implement linkage and hydraulic control helps you do better planting, easier.

In only a minute or two, you can attach the planter to the tractor. Going to and from the field, it is raised high off the ground in transport position. Depth is set hydraulically by a touch on the hydraulic control lever. *Features:* Sword type opener. Seed cells that fit. Stirring action to prevent seed bridging over cells. Two depths of cells. Hoppers tip over for emptying and cleaning. Three sets of plates furnished. Row widths adjustable from 28" to 44". 20" open center press wheels. *Extra Equipment:* Marker, duplex hoppers, fertilizer attachment, plates for wide variety of seed.

Planter is raised to transport position and depth adjusted by finger-tip hydraulic control.

Fertilizer attachment, designed for accurate placement, is easily put on or taken off.

Litho. in U. S. A.

This literature details what's called the Ferguson "drill type" corn planter. It was supposed to provide faster planting than was possible with the older check-row planters.

the Blue River. A new plant was built in 1898, and in 1965, the business came under new ownership and the name was changed to Dempster Industries, Inc.

In addition to pumps and windmills, Dempster was an early manufacturer of farm implements. In 1899 the company brought out an innovative design known as the Low-Down Grain Drill. It was far superior to other available seeding machines of the time, and was followed in 1900 by the first practical and efficient two-row cultivator. The next 60 years brought a series of new planting and cultivating implements from Dempster, including the deep-furrow grain drill, planters, and cultivators based on the single-unit concept. This allowed row spacing to be easily adapted to field requirements. Dempster cooperated with the University of Nebraska in 1960 to design and produce the first practical minimum-till planter.

During 1942 to 1944, the company helped in the war effort by manufacturing 90-millimeter shells. Dempster developed a planter attachment to fit the Ferguson middlebuster frame before 1942, and the total production of this planter was sold to a Ferguson distributor, O'Shea-Rogers of Lincoln, Nebraska.

Other Dempster implements had also been adapted to the three-point hitch and sold through Ferguson distributors in the Central Plains states, earning Dempster an excellent reputation. Yet it wasn't until December 1942 that Ferguson became interested in Dempster as a supplier.

At that time, O'Shea-Rogers introduced the two parties. Ferguson's Merritt Hill evaluated the prospects of a business relationship and gave Dempster a good report. But further talks revealed Dempster had no production capacity beyond its war production quota to cover implements for Ferguson. Dempster was favorable to a postwar deal, though, and in the meantime would try to get new allotments or reassign existing allotments.

Dempster and Ferguson Strike a Deal

In April 1943, a deal was struck for Dempster to make lister cultivators, lister planters, duckfoot tillers, and attachments under the Fer-

These are Ford photographs of yet another type of two-row lister planter.

guson name. In the meantime, Ferguson engineers tested Dempster products and found little that needed changing. Negotiations continued between the two companies over a couple of points. One was a Ferguson proposal for production requirements exceeding the capacity of Dempster's farm implement division. When Ferguson asked Dempster to expand its facilities, the company purchased a new building. Also being negotiated at the time was a contract between the two companies. It's believed that a standard Ferguson contract, with minor changes, was to run for five years beginning October 1945.

Because neither Ferguson nor Dempster held WPB quotas for planters, no Ferguson planters were produced in 1943 or 1944. Production got under way in 1945, and Ferguson took delivery of approximately 6,000 planters during the first 9 months of 1946.

Relative to the Dearborn-Ferguson conference of May 1947, these implement orders were in the hands of Dempster for July 1947 through June 1948 production:

Grain drill
3,000
Rotary moldboard lister
1,500
Planter attachments
4,800
Lister cultivator
2,400
Miscellaneous tiller attachments,
    press wheels
  6,000

Dearborn initially contacted Dempster in January 1947. The direct quotes give an idea of an almost cat-and-mouse veiled effort at diplomacy on the part of both Dearborn and Dempster during a time when the industry was most assuredly aware of the split between Ferguson and Ford. The industry also knew that Ferguson was having trouble securing financing for tractor production. In a January 22, 1947, letter to Dempster, a Dearborn employee wrote:

. . . requesting information as to whether Dempster manufactured implements for use with the Ford tractor, mentioning that, as he probably read in the paper, Dearborn planned to have a complete line of implements to merchandise with the Ford tractor and that at a later date we shall get in touch with you regarding a personal visit. In the meantime, any time you are in Detroit we shall be pleased to have you call on us.

Dempster replied on January 24 that it was manufacturing implements:

. . . for use on the Fordson [sic] tractor but that we are under contractual arrangements with Ferguson which will continue beyond July 1, 1947. This being the case, we are not in a position to pledge more of our productive capacity for the manufacture of farm implements and farm implement attachments for tractor use.

Somewhat of a hybrid, this unit combines two Ferguson implements: A ridger frame onto which a potato planter has been mounted, plus a seat for an operator.

Dearborn Looks to Specialize

By late spring or early summer 1947, Dearborn had made arrangements for most of what it considered essential implements. Now it was ready to turn attention to more specialized items to round out its line. At this time, Dempster was considered a desired source for lister planters, cultivators, and duckfoot attachments. In June, Harry Ferguson, Inc., President Roger Kyes reported that Dempster had requested modification of the contract to give Dempster a guaranteed minimum dollar volume and certain other changes. Dempster was no doubt experiencing the same dilemma as other Ferguson suppliers. Ferguson at the time was cutting back orders and suspending acceptance of deliveries of product. It's easy to understand from a business perspective the dilemma of Dempster and other manufacturers. It was Dempster's intention to honor the contract with Ferguson. But some of these manufacturers had already made commitments to expand their plants, hire additional personnel, and make other investments in time and money.

In June, Dempster approached Ferguson for modification of the contract. The Ferguson board took the position "that in no event should the Company give up its nonexclusive license on Dempster items."

However, the passing of another month had intensified Ferguson's deteriorating position. By July 24, 1947, Dempster had obtained a release from Ferguson allowing Dempster to supply Dearborn with the requested implements.

Lister planters and cultivators are produced in the fall and winter so they're available for field work the following spring. With the Ferguson release in hand by July, production should have started immediately. Dearborn engineering approval was delayed, and Dearborn's first purchase orders were issued to Dempster much later, in January 1948. The exact number of implements ordered and delivered isn't known. It's believed that during the first three months of 1948, Dearborn's Dempster production was 4,500 units, mostly lister planters. It's also unclear if Ferguson continued to receive any implements after the modification of the contract in July, although it's assumed the company did.

A last note regarding Dempster planters and cultivators from the "Memorandum for files": "Since the implements Dempster sold to Ferguson and the ones sold to Dearborn are almost, if not wholly, identical, the service parts Dearborn will furnish its dealers will be usable on any Dempster implement, whether sold through Dearborn or Ferguson."

One last company should be mentioned in connection with planters. In 1946, Standard Steel Company, Kansas City, Missouri, was producing corn planters for Ferguson. The only additional information available on this company is that it also manufactured the Ferguson tractor jack for K-P Manufacturing Company, Olathe, Kansas. It isn't much, but it deserves mention.

CHAPTER NINE

Harrows, Rotary Hoes, and Weeders

FARM TOOLS INC. SUPPLIES FERGUSON

This Ferguson fully mounted tandem disc has adjustable gangs. The two levers are used to adjust the cutting angle of the disc, depending on soil conditions or how much dirt the operator wants to move.

Disc harrow procurement and production highlight the difficulties surrounding Ford-Ferguson implement production during three critical periods.

First, initial implement design in 1938 and production during 1939 posed a somewhat greater engineering challenge than that of the tractor. Putting even the basic implements into the line required continued adaptation and ingenuity over several years. Also, seldom did production satisfy demand.

A second critical period was the war years. Material restrictions constantly kept production in arrears of demand. Again it took great effort and ingenuity, this time of a different nature, to maintain enough raw materials for even the basic manufacturing needs. Couple this with the quota system, which determined which products, and how many of them, a given manufacturer could produce, reducing many production lines to a "start and stop" schedule.

Added to this was the manpower shortage faced by most factories. And the material shortages continued for some time after the war.

A third period that was traumatic for Ford-Ferguson three-point implement development occurred through the time leading up to, during, and immediately after the demise of the Ford and Ferguson agreement. Farmers pressed dealers. Dealers hounded distributors. Distributors impatiently waited

In contrast to the fully mounted tandem this 7-foot Ferguson disc is a pull type disc hooked up to the three-point hitch of the tractor. When the lift arms of the tractor raise up, the disk gangs straighten out to make it easier for the operator to make turns. When the lift arms are dropped again at the completion of the turn, the disc returns to its preset angle.

for deliveries—from whom and of what they couldn't be certain.

In the case of the disc harrow, a strange but effective deterrent to production was the apparent scarcity of discs. More than one communication of the period cites this shortage as a factor in slowing units for shipment. One frustrated production manager returned a letter to the Ferguson organization suggesting, with no little feeling, that it find its own discs, and if it could, the successful searcher was certainly a better man than he.

Some events concerning disc harrows and spring-tooth harrows in 1946 and 1947 have an interesting tie to 1925—the year the Sherman brothers joined up with Harry Ferguson to manufacture duplex plows for the Fordson tractor in Evansville, Indiana. Ferguson-Sherman,

Inc., initially contracted the Vulcan Plow Company to produce the plow. Roderick Lean was also involved as the producer of the duplex plows. Various records and documents indicate that both of these companies, as well as Ferguson-Sherman, went out of business in the mid- to late 1920s or early 1930s.

The "New" Ferguson-Sherman

Ferguson-Sherman managed to remain afloat until replaced by Ferguson-Sherman Manufacturing Company of Dearborn, Michigan. George Sherman was the first procurement officer, by function if not by title, for Ferguson-Sherman Manufacturing. The company was formed to handle the distribution of Ford-Ferguson tractors and implements, and Sherman was directly involved in the Ford plow effort at the Rouge plant.

As early as 1939, while the 9N tractor was still under development, a farm implement manufacturer in Evansville, Indiana, obtained details of the hydraulic lift and hitch linkage. The company immediately began to redesign some of its existing implements for use with the new tractor. There's little doubt that this firm, Farm Tools, Inc., learned of the new tractor development through George Sherman, who undoubtedly had many business contacts in the Evansville area.

Farm Tools, Inc., was incorporated in 1930 after a merger of Vulcan Plow Company and

This is a close-up of the hitch of the pull-type Ferguson tandem disc.

What you see is what you get with this Dearborn disc, because the angle of cut isn't adjustable. Dearborn made two nonadjustable disc models, of which this is the first.

Roderick Lean Company. Both of these companies were hurt badly when Ford stopped production of the Fordson tractor. Some of the "hurt" probably was due to their business dealings with Ferguson-Sherman, Inc., which also staggered by the withdrawal of the Fordson.

Could this be testimony to the trust these companies had in George Sherman? Might it also be an effort by Sherman to give these people a chance to recoup some of their losses by giving them an opportunity for future business?

Two additional companies were involved in the merger that created Farm Tools: Hayes Pump & Planter Company and Peoria Drill and Seeder Company. Farm Tools operated all the merged companies as divisions.

Plows and plow parts were manufactured at the Evansville plant, while the Mansfield, Ohio, plant, which housed the general offices, was the manufacturing location of disc harrows, spring-tooth harrows, rotary hoes, and various other implements. Farm Tools is credited with many substantial contributions to mounted equipment designs during the entire period of N-Series tractor production. The firm's tandem disc was non-mounted, although the single disc was mounted. The implement engineer of Farm Tools held a patent covering the angling mechanism on the tandem disc harrow, and he contributed many other important design elements as well.

Terms of the Agreement

Just how the "patent by others, and used by Ferguson" arrangement worked is illustrated by this May 1, 1941, legal document titled, "Memorandum of Agreement" between Farm Tools, Inc., and Ferguson-Sherman Manufacturing Corporation:

The parties have heretofore cooperated and are continuing to cooperate in the development of disc harrows adaptable for use in connection with the Ford Tractor-Ferguson System. Second party [Ferguson-Sherman] has promoted and agrees to endeavor to continue to promote and develop sales outlets for such of said disc harrows as shall be mutually agreed upon by both parties.

In consideration of the advantages which will accrue to first party [Farm Tools] as a result of the activities of the parties as above set forth, first party agrees that if it obtains any patents upon disc harrows for which sales outlets have been heretofore or are hereafter so developed by second party, it will and hereby does grant to second party a nonexclusive royalty-free license thereunder throughout the world. Such license shall be effective for the full life of the patents, even though active cooperation and relations between the parties shall at any time terminate. Except for such license, first party shall retain full title to such patents and all other rights and equities therein and thereunder.

This isn't an unusual document. What it shows is how Ferguson was able to use the patented implement features of other companies on Ferguson equipment. Note that the engineering departments of both parties were cooperating on implement design. This is also proof that there was already two years of cooperation between the two companies. Farm Tools undoubtedly performed the bulk of the engineering tasks, while Ferguson's staff held the right to make suggestions, and also exercised the right of approval or rejection of subsequent designs. Records show that Farm Tools owned all production tooling for the tandem disc harrow.

Because of the financial losses suffered when Ford stopped production of the Fordson, Farm Tools management was extremely wary of anything connected with Ford Motor Company. In addition, it's more than likely that Farm Tools management was also not overly fond of Ferguson executives Kyes and Horace D'Angelo.

Farm Tools was a well-managed and successful company that would like, but didn't need, Ferguson's business, so it could be somewhat hardline when it came to the written agreements.

Ferguson Shows Its Business Savvy

How then did Ferguson obtain the patent license and the cooperation of the Farm Tools engineering department? Quite simply, Ferguson outflanked and outmaneuvered Farm Tools. Ferguson went to the WPB and managed to

Howard Howell, Dover, Ohio, with his nonadjustable Dearborn tandem disc.

It was said that the Dearborn rotary hoe could also be used as a weeder. However, its action was so active that the implement was seldom used for this purpose and was instead utilized for general-purpose cultivation.

obtain classification as the "producer" of implements manufactured for it by Farm Tools. Ferguson was able to use this leverage to insist on certain concessions from Farm Tools, because it was only through Ferguson that materials were available for production. Farm Tools wasn't the only supplier caught in this dilemma. From Ferguson's view, what he did just made good business sense. Here's the perspective as taken from a Ferguson publication, *History of the Company*:

At the very outset of limitations on production by the War Production Board, our company took aggressive action at Washington to get Harry Ferguson, Inc., established as the "producer" on those items which we justly felt should be called our own. We were successful in getting recognition as a "producer" on certain items from the War Production Board with the result that we own and control the quota on the Tractor and [such implements].

In spite of all the corporate posturing, which is often part of big business, disc harrows were eventually produced at Farm Tools, but not without further difficulties. Manufacturing production suffered greatly as the U.S. committed more and more men to the war effort. The situation became so acute that in 1944, Merritt Hill of Ferguson's procurement department began recruiting laborers for the Farm Tools production line.

A memo from Hill to Ferguson President Roger Kyes stated that the manpower situation at Evansville was improving and they had already hired 17 women. The intent was to staff the line with all-female help that wouldn't be called up for war service. Though not as glamorous as Rosie the Riveter building airplanes, the situation prompted one Farm Tools employee to comment about quality, about which Ferguson gave them re-occurring fits, "After all, it's a plow and not an airplane they're making."

Actual production records of the early years are lacking. It's likely, though, that Farm Tools tandem disc harrows were available in limited quantities by late 1940 or early 1941. We do know that Farm Tools supplied plow bases to Ford in 1939. Plows were a much higher priority than disc harrows, even though work was being done on harrow design as early as 1939. It's not until the first half of 1943 that we know for sure that Ferguson purchased 2,046 disc harrows from Farm Tools. In the first half of 1944, the same year women were placed on the line, Ferguson purchased 12,695 disc harrows.

In January 1946, Ferguson placed an order for 25,000 tandem disc harrows. This order was downsized to 10,000, as the Ford-Ferguson split was pending. Ferguson's relationship with Farm Tools paralleled events during the period with his other suppliers: Cut back orders, pay whatever penalty necessary, and then take delivery of small numbers on an uncertain schedule.

Negotiations Follow a Pattern

Of course, Dearborn approached Farm Tools as a possible supplier of implements for the Dearborn line. The negotiations followed a preset pattern for both Ferguson and Dearborn: Ferguson tried to hang on, refused to release Farm Tools from its contract, retrenched, and finally succumbed to the irresistible circumstances. By May 1947, Farm Tools had agreed to join the Dearborn supply network, and it appears that Farm Tools reserved enough production capacity to supply Ferguson, too.

Implements made in this period included the tandem disc harrow (drag type with hydraulic adjustment of gangs), spring-tooth harrow, and rotary hoe. The single disc harrow (mounted) had been offered in the Ferguson line. It's not believed this implement was part of the Dearborn picture at this time. Dearborn purchase orders were issued calling for delivery of tandem discs at the rate of 200 a week beginning September 8, 1947. Delivery of spring-tooth harrows began November–December 1947. Rotary hoes listed delivery as September–December 1947.

A letter from the period when Farm Tools and Dearborn first agreed to do business notes "All parts on Farm Tools' disc harrows are interchangeable with Ferguson parts."

And, a later letter says, "All parts on the rotary hoe and two-section spring-tooth harrow are interchangeable with those which we formerly produced for our other customer."

This is a spike-tooth harrow that Ford used in its advertising.

The other customer was obviously Ferguson.

Dearborn got its supplier. It didn't get a marriage made in heaven, though. Farm Tools couldn't produce enough implements to meet Dearborn demands. Farm Tools offered to double production on the tandem disc harrow if Dearborn could furnish disc blades for the extra production. It isn't clear if this was ever accomplished, although it seems that Dearborn had already exhausted its ingenuity in obtaining disc blades.

In late 1947, Farm Tools was for sale and Dearborn hoped to be the buyer. While Dearborn management was awaiting advice of counsel on how the purchase of Farm Tools might affect the *Ferguson v. Ford* lawsuit, Schott Brothers, Cleveland, Ohio, stepped in and purchased Farm Tools. Around this same time, Farm Rite, also a supplier of Ferguson and Dearborn tandem disc harrows, gave notice to Dearborn that due to unfavorable labor conditions, it was discontinuing the manufacture of farm implements.

It seems that the immediate production problems on disc harrows was addressed by diverting production facilities and materials from the Farm Tools general line to three-point implements and/or by moving part of the production over to other Schott-owned plants in the Cleveland area. What is certain is that at the same time Dearborn was hit with a 10 percent price increase.

Remember that a sizable portion of Ferguson production was being exported. Most assuredly during the war years this was part of the Lend-Lease program, although this program ceased in 1945. However, a letter from Farm Tools to Ferguson in November 1947 reported that 2,700 double disc harrows were released for export. At the same time 919 were released for domestic shipment.

All we know about the Alexander Manufacturing Company is that it was listed as a supplier for the bush and bog disc harrow. Perhaps the Alexander Manufacturing Company supplied notched discs to be fitted on certain models of disc harrows to convert them to use in applications that required such discs.

Rotary Hoe

The one source for rotary hoes from the inception of the 9N through the beginning of Dearborn's initial purchasing efforts was Farm Tools, Inc., which manufactured rotary hoes for sale through its distribution network before its affiliation with Ferguson. This implement probably followed the same evolutionary process as others that were modified to fit the three-point linkage.

A rotary hoe wasn't considered one of the five or six most important implements to offer with the N-Series tractor. So it didn't receive the

Ford utilized this photographs of the nonadjustable disc in its promotional materials.

same engineering attention that plows, mowers, cultivators, and disc harrows attracted.

Ferguson hadn't developed a rotary hoe before 1939. Nor was it one of the implements brought to the United States for the Henry Ford demonstration. Nor was it offered at the debut of the 9N tractor. No doubt its first appearance was sometime after 1943.

A 1943 memo lists three items that Ferguson desired to have engineered for mounted attachment: spring-tooth harrows, spike-tooth harrows, and rotary hoes. Ferguson's engineers replied that these items wouldn't be available for some time since they were currently working on 16 other implements. Unfortunately, they didn't list the other 16 implements. Farm Tools was then asked to have its engineering department develop these implements and submit models to Ferguson for testing. Little documentation has survived that sheds further light on these three items.

A safe conclusion is that Farm Tools was responsible for the total job of developing these implements. If previous guidelines were followed, Ferguson's engineering department would have had final approval or rejection of the design. The best information available places first production of rotary hoes some time in 1945. The earliest reference to rotary hoe production numbers is found in records of the Ferguson-Dearborn meeting of May 1947. Ferguson's rotary hoe orders for delivery during the last half of 1947 were listed at 3,000.

Because of Ferguson's deteriorating situation in late 1946 and early 1947, he was forced to cancel many orders to Farm Tools. It's believed that he either canceled the rotary hoe order completely or that it was fulfilled completely.

The latter doesn't seem likely, because by July 18, Farm Tools had orally committed its production to Dearborn. The explanation for

the Farm Tools decision to align with Dearborn was based on both Ferguson's cancellations and the failure to submit a projection for additional implement requirements.

Weeders

Weeders should be one of the simplest implements to design and engineer. Ford-Dearborn engineers estimated only a few months would be necessary for this effort. Perhaps the simplicity was deceptive. At any rate, Dearborn's weeder design caused considerable embarrassment to the company a few months after it was first marketed.

Weeders weren't a priority implement for either Ferguson or Dearborn in its efforts to establish their "lines" of mounted implements. No weeder was offered in any volume until 1942 or 1943.

Both Ferguson and Dearborn had only one manufacturer for weeders, Central Architectural

This rotary hoe photographs was used by Ford in advertising.

Iron Works, Chicago, Illinois. At the time (1939) the company was owned by E. J. Schmitz, who had several business interests in the Chicago area. Until 1942, its business was solely fabrication of structural steel products. Central, reaching the conclusion shared by many other companies, believed it needed to diversify to better survive the postwar glut of manufacturing facilities that would be competing for business.

In 1947, Central separated its farm implement manufacturing division and put it into a new corporation operating under the name of Farm Rite Implement Company. Technically, any implements manufactured for Ferguson before the new company was incorporated would come from Central Architectural Iron Works. Dearborn's version of the same implement would be a Farm Rite product. To lessen confusion, assume both companies were supplied by Farm Rite Implement Company.

Farm Rite's desire to diversify led it to the Ferguson organization with the offer to tool up and produce whatever implements Ferguson needed. Ferguson surely needed manufacturing support, but at this time the manufacturing capabilities would be worthless without WPB quotas of materials for implements.

Ferguson Gains a Harrow Manufacturer

The luck of the Irish again prevailed. Ferguson found and bought a Minnesota company called the John Kovar Company. Included in the sale was Kovar's inventory, spring-tooth harrow manufacturing rights, and WPB quotas. Harrow production and tooling was moved immediately to the Farm Rite factory, and in 1942, Farm Rite made its first venture into the implement manufacturing business with disc harrows. Weeders would soon follow.

Ferguson's first weeder supplier was the B. F. Avery Company, which produced a redesign of its standard weeder to fit the Ferguson three-point linkage. Avery wouldn't grant any of its implement quota to Ferguson, but agreed to allow other manufacturers to make the weeder for Ferguson. There's some evidence that Farm Tools made the weeder for Ferguson. However, if this was the case it probably wasn't for long. Regardless of the source, the numbers produced would have been low.

Under the same agreement with Avery, Farm Rite became Ferguson's main supplier of weeders. Production numbers are available only for the first nine months of 1946, during which time Ferguson's weeder sales reached 6,100 units. Farm Rite never really managed to develop its farm implement division into a successful operation, even though its dealings with Ferguson led to production of the tandem disc,

Ferguson-Sherman four-row weeder was designed to disturb just the top few inches of soil in planted crops in order to halt early weed growth before the crops emerged from the soil. It was possible to get over a lot of ground in a hurry with this implement, because it can be used at a field speed almost as fast as the operator could tolerate. The two end sections fold up for passing through gates or while traveling on narrow lanes.

the rear-mounted mower, the spring-tooth harrow, and the weeder during 1942 through 1944. The company was also engaged in development of a corn picker. This work consumed considerable time and money.

In 1945, Ferguson began to withdraw implements from Farm Rite production. By year's end, the weeder was the only Ferguson production item left. Dearborn's approach to Farm Rite was predictable, and in 1947, Dearborn had 12,000 weeders on order for delivery during the last six months of the year. Sales of weeders slowed to a halt after only 2,300 had been delivered, inducing Dearborn to cancel 8,000 of the 12,000 order.

Dearborn was soon to discover a possible, and embarrassing, reason why sales had plummeted. Someone brought it to Dearborn's attention that the weeder it advertised and sold as a "four-row weeder" was actually only 11-feet wide. Farmers may not have engineering degrees, but they darn sure know whether the implement is working two rows or four rows of crops.

Approximately 2,400 of the undersized weeders had been sold. Management issued a stop-work order on all weeders in production, then suggested that work efforts be directed toward developing a true four-row weeder. It also suggested that the units already in the hands of customers be retrofitted with wider outer sections. Whether this was ever done isn't confirmed in any documents.

Ferguson's weeders were 13 feet, 4 inches wide compared to Dearborn's 11 feet. Whether intentionally or by coincidence, the price of both was exactly the same.

Weeders were essential to the mounted implement line. Yet they weren't a high-dollar or high-volume item, so they weren't a real money-maker for manufacturer or marketer.

When Dearborn cut back and eventually canceled the balance of its 12,000-unit order, Farm Rite and Dearborn found themselves in the position of having material and production facilities to supply three times the weeders needed for several years. This was in sharp contrast to other implements that were always begging for material and production.

After this development, Farm Rite magnanimously offered to supply Ferguson with weeders any time weeders were needed.

Records confirm that Dearborn continued purchasing weeders in small quantities during 1948. In all probability, Farm Rite also supplied Ferguson at this time.

The sales leaflet describes the advantages of the four-row weeder as accurate depth control, adjustable width, and strength combined with flexibility.

Ferguson-Sherman

FOUR-ROW WEEDER

For Low Cost Weed Control

Endless hours can be saved by the Ferguson-Sherman Four-row Weeder which is designed to take full advantage of the many benefits offered by the Ford tractor with Ferguson system.

The accurate depth control of this unit implement permits its use over growing crops . . . before they come through the soil . . . and until they are 12″ to 14″ high.

Its springy, sharp teeth provide a zig-zagging agitation that tears out the small weeds and turns their roots up to the sun and wind, before they have a chance to rob moisture and nourishment from the crop. At the same time, it does an excellent job of mulching hard-baked top soil, without leaving the small indentations common to other tools developed for this type of work.

This weeder is used for cultivating such crops as corn, cotton, potatoes, soy beans, beets . . . in fact, practically every crop where weed control is a problem. It is also frequently used in the preparation of a fine seed bed for truck crops . . . and for breaking up the soil crust on winter wheat and other small grains.

The large acreage that can be covered in a day . . . the wide variety of crops which can be handled . . . the reduction of time which would have to be spent with other cultivating methods . . . and the resulting increased yields . . . make the Ferguson-Sherman Four-row Weeder one of the most useful and valuable investments to be made for weed control.

SEE REVERSE SIDE FOR CONSTRUCTION DETAILS

CHAPTER TEN

Blades, Dozers, Scoops, Loaders, and More

ADDITIONAL IMPLEMENTS A TO Z

A beautifully restored Ford 8N tractor complements an immaculate front-mounted Arps Corporation Model LJ-3 "Blackhawk" snowplow. It's similar to the Dearborn Model 19-2 angledozer. The 27-inch-high blade has a cutting width of 60 inches. The blade can be manually moved into any position from extreme left to extreme right. SP-19 side plates, not shown, were an optional accessory and couldn't be used for side plowing. BMS-1 adjustable skid shoes, not shown, were also available.

The industrial-strength Overland Scraper was made by the Western Equipment Manufacturing Co., Glendale, California. It was expressly designed and built to work with the Ford tractor fingertip control. Weighing 1,050 pounds, the scraper had a level capacity of 27 cubic feet and a heaped capacity of 35 cubic feet.

A name commonly seen on blades and snowplows for the three-point system is the Arps Corporation of New Holstein, Wisconsin, a company founded in 1920 by Bruno Arps.

The Arps half-track accessory for Ford-Ferguson wheels has an interesting ancestral lineage. In the 1920s when the mail "always" had to go through regardless of the deep snow, the Arps Corporation designed and built a snowmobile conversion for the Ford car. The design was similar to the tractor half-tracks, on which the tracks were driven by the car's rear wheels but the front wheels were fitted with skis. Approximately 15,000 of these "snowmobiles" were produced.

A road grader designed for other tractor makes was also a predecessor to a similar line of equipment for the N-Series tractors.

Arps approached Ferguson-Sherman in 1939, and before the end of the year a deal was struck that made Arps products available through Ford distributors and dealers. This was an exceptionally quick entry into the market.

All designs and blueprints originated with the Arps engineering department, but as usual, Ferguson had final approval of any new designs or design changes.

The line of industrial equipment called "Blackhawk" included snowplows, bulldozers, angledozers, road graders, pick-up scrapers, scar-ifiers, power winches (double and single drum), dragline equipment, power loaders, and cordwood saws.

The company remained a family business until 1963, when it merged with the Chromalloy American Corporation. It became a division of the Ameriquip Corporation in 1980. Today the company specializes in producing commercial loaders, backhoes, posthole diggers, and more. Many of its current products are manufactured for companies such as Deere & Company, Ford, and Bush Hog.

Arps became a Dearborn supplier and sold exclusively to Dearborn after the Ford-Ferguson split. The equipment was painted gray for Ferguson and red for Dearborn. The Arps name wasn't on the equipment; instead there was only the identification plate of either Ferguson or Dearborn. The original plant in New Holstein is still a manufacturing facility today, along with a plant located in Keil, Wisconsin.

In addition to its other implements, Towner Manufacturing Company of Santa Ana, California, manufactured and supplied a front end loader, trip dump scraper, buck scraper, and land leveler.

Another supplier of blades who joined the supplier network in 1944 or 1945 was the Carrington Manufacturing Company of Fulton, Missouri. There's evidence that the company also manufactured a posthole digger, disc terracer, and planter.

The agreement between Ferguson and Carrington contained one novel clause that apparently wasn't in any other Ferguson contracts. The agreement stated that George E. Carrington was to be paid $500 a month in advance for the duration of the agreement. The agreement had the usual one-year cancellation clause.

The $500 a month payment was for "representing himself to have unique skill as an engineer for the development and invention of farm and industrial machinery, accessories, equipment, and the like." Any patentable inventions were to be filed for and owned by Ferguson.

Carrington was to be given first consideration as the actual manufacturer of any products Ferguson approved for manufacture. Ferguson held the right to withhold such manufacturing rights if he considered the Carrington facility inadequate for such manufacturing.

Additional Implements and Accessories

Ford engineer Harold Brock offers this observation about the N-Series tractor and its accompanying implements and accessories:

I think there's one thing interesting about the little tractor. As time went on more and more field people found uses for the tractor and made special implements for it. Some independent made a little jack where you put it underneath the front axle, rear axle, and hooked it on a hydraulic lift and the tractor lifted itself off the ground to change tread widths. So you almost had to give the industry credit for doing a lot of innovative work to make the little tractor more popular.

This chapter covers some of those industry developments, including implements and accessories sold through the Ferguson and/or Dearborn networks.

Jack

The jack that Brock mentioned could rightfully be held up as the biggest "tempest in a teapot" surrounding both Ferguson's and Dearborn's procurement efforts. Manufacturers by the score were climbing on the 9N bandwagon. They were hoping to be part of Ford's next Model T, trusting that their invention would lead to their own fortune on the coattails of Ford and Ferguson.

Tom Poor, an eccentric, self-styled inventor from Olathe, Kansas, jumped into the frenzy in 1940 with the K-P tractor jack. Poor, along with John E. Kisinger and Herman T. Kisinger, filed for United States Letters Patent on the jack on August 22, 1940. These three individuals at one

Dearborn Manufacturing marketed this industrial-strength grader for mounting on the 8N tractor. Dwight Emstrom, Galesburg, Illinois, restored both the grader and the tractor.

time or another were involved in other business in the Olathe community, including a Hudson automobile agency, a Ferguson dealership, and a Dearborn dealership. Their jack business operated under the name K-P Manufacturing Company, although it maintained no manufacturing facilities. Standard Steel Company of Kansas City, Missouri, manufactured the jack and is believed to have owned the production tooling.

There's good evidence that the K-P jack was sold directly to Ferguson dealers as early as 1940. It was a most useful accessory to help space wheels or change tires. Merritt Hill wrote that Harry Ferguson, Inc., should con-

The Dearborn blade can completely swivel through 360 degrees. The operator is able to remain in his tractor seat while reaching back to pull the long rod that controls blade angle.

This early Dearborn scoop is nonreversible. It can only be operated while moving forward or stopped. Later models could be hooked to the tractor facing either forward or backward. Facing backward, they could be backed into a pile of dirt, something that wasn't always possible while driving forward.

sider seeking distribution rights on the item. This wasn't acted on until 1945, probably because it was a rather low priority compared to other implements.

Actually there were two styles of Ferguson jacks. One type mounted under the rear axle, while the other mounted under where the bottom two links attached to the axle housing. The first style couldn't be used on the 8N tractor.

While no copy of the contract between Ferguson and K-P is available, records contain a March 1947 letter from K-P to Ferguson canceling its contract—presumably a contract that had given Ferguson exclusive distribution rights for its jack. Ferguson's reply refers to the contract, but at the time declined to sign a release. And a stellar IQ isn't required to deduce the reason K-P was asking for a release from the contract: Ferguson's sales were down, and orders were being canceled or deferred when Dearborn entered the picture.

The Ford-Ferguson tractor jack wasn't an essential piece of equipment for a tractor owner, yet it was a most handy item to have around. In fact, owning a K-P jack became almost a fad. Hill remembers that a jack went out with almost every tractor:

I know that we were always hearing about and seeing those jacks in the field, but it wasn't considered an important enough item for us to bother with. It was after I left for the West Coast that Poor and Ferguson made a deal. I don't remember having been in any negotiations of any kind with Tom Poor.

But after I got on the West Coast we really had tractor jacks in quantity. I remember that they were coming out of our ears. We finally got to a point where the distributors were shipping one with every tractor, apparently due to Ferguson efforts to increase its accessory sales volumes.

At first glance "a jack for every tractor" appears to fall into the category of exaggeration for effect. Production on 9N and 2N tractors reached almost 300,000 by this time. That would be an awful lot of jacks. But these jacks

1946 Harry Ferguson, Inc. Report

The following information is taken from a 1946 report on Harry Ferguson, Inc., conducted by the firm of McKinsey, Kearney & Company, Chicago, Illinois. The implements are listed as classified by the Bureau of the Census:

Plows and Listers

Ferguson sells the following implements:
- Two-bottom 12-inch sod clay base plow
- Two-bottom 12-inch slot base plow
- Two-bottom 14-inch stubble base plow
- One-bottom 16-inch general-purpose plow
- One-bottom 18-inch general-purpose plow
- One-bottom 16-inch two-way plow
- One-bottom disc plow
- Two-bottom disc plow
- Three-bottom disc plow
- Subsoil plow
- Disc terracer
- Blade terracer
- Tiller
- Fertilizer attachment for plows
- Soil scoop

Harrows, Rollers, Pulverizers, and Stalk Cutters

- Six-foot tandem disc harrow
- Single-disc harrow
- Offset-disc harrow
- Two-row stalk cutter
- Spring-tooth harrow
- Rigid-frame spring-tooth harrow, field cultivator type

A spike-tooth harrow is ready for production. No land roller, pulverizer, or packer is yet in production.

Planting, Seeding, and Fertilizer Machinery

- High-speed corn drill
- Lister planters, with fertilizer attachments
- Grain drill with seeder and fertilizer attachment
- Manure spreaders
- Manure loaders
- Fertilizer distributor

The principal items not yet sold by Ferguson are check-row corn planters, potato planters, garden and vegetable planters, transplanters, broadcast seeders, and lime spreaders.

Cultivators and Weeders

- Lister cultivator
- Spring-tooth cultivator, rear-mounted
- Solid-tooth cultivator, rear-mounted
- Four-row weeder
- Rotary hoe

We encountered considerable resistance to the rear-mounted cultivator. The possible replacement by a conventional front-mounted type, where the operator can see the cultivator in operation, is under consideration.

Harvesting Machinery

In the harvesting machinery classification, Ferguson at present offers only a one-row corn picker. The Woods Brothers corn picker sold exclusively by Ferguson is considered to be an excellent machine. The following implements aren't yet sold by Ferguson, but several are in process of development or testing:
- Combine
- Grain and rice binders
- Potato digger and picker
- Beet harvester and loader
- Windrowers and swathers

weren't difficult to build, and considering Standard's production capabilities, these numbers may not be unrealistic. The company could and did run two shifts during times of high demand. It could produce between 9,000 and 10,000 units a month, and was considering establishing satellite facilities on the West Coast and in Canada. And there are some indications that large numbers of these jacks were also shipped to England. Demand for these jacks

exposes a side of Harry Ferguson that seems beneath his usual standards of business ethics.

Poor and his partners didn't have patent protection outside of the United States, and Ferguson, or an employee of his organization, took specifications and drawings of the K-P jack to England and began manufacturing the jack there. Later it was learned that the patent on the K-P jack was virtually indefensible, according to Dearborn attorneys. So maybe it wasn't bad busi-

ness ethics on Ferguson's part, but good business tactics instead.

Making and selling tractor jacks, nevertheless, was small business in the overall scheme of things. Ferguson paid approximately $7 apiece for the jacks, and he retailed them for approximately $15. If you consider all the people getting a slice of that $15—Standard had to manufacture the jack and hopefully make a profit, K-P of course wanted a cut for its patent royalty, Ferguson needed a share,

- Corn and cane binders
- Peanut, pea, and bean harvesters
- Forage harvesters

Ferguson withdrew the Woods Brothers 6-foot combine from the market because it needed further development.

Haying Machinery
- Highway mower, side-mounted
- Rear-mounted mower
- Sweep rake

The principal implements in this group not sold by Ferguson are:
- Side-delivery rake
- Stackers
- Balers
- Hay loaders

Machines for Preparing Crops for Market or for Use
No items in this group are sold yet by Ferguson except a small number of feed mills. A hammer mill is under test.

Farm Wagons, Trucks and Other Farm Transportation Equipment
- Two-wheel farm trailer, 3-ton
- Four-wheel wagon
- Two-wheel transport

In general, it can be said that the line is sufficiently complete in the basic implements to permit the company to compete successfully and to complement the tractor in an adequate manner since it has been proved that it is extremely difficult to sell tractors without a complementary line of implements. The company has been spending considerable time and money in the engineering, development, and testing of new and improved products.

distributors wanted to make money, and the dealers were also hopeful of a profit. And, since it appears many of the jacks were thrown in as part of the tractor deal, business was booming but obviously nobody was getting rich.

Perhaps because everyone seemed to want the K-P jack, Tom Poor believed he was in a strong bargaining position with Dearborn when it came calling for jacks. The eccentric "jack man" of Kansas called Dearborn's bluff.

K-P wanted a price increase and other contractual concessions from Dearborn, whose reaction was not to even bother about the darn things, under the assumption the distributors had enough jacks to last them for 10 years. Dearborn's further assumption was that the Ferguson jacks for the 9N and 2N would fit the 8N. They wouldn't.

To everyone's amazement Dearborn distributors started requesting a fresh supply of jacks in late summer of 1947. Dearborn approached K-P about the new development, including offering engineering help to fit the jack to the 8N. Poor, who handled most of K-P's negotiations, replied that they weren't interested and would market the jacks directly to dealers and distributors themselves. This runs counter to most instances in which Dearborn consistently got the suppliers it wanted and, in most cases, on its terms. Dearborn wasn't about to let a small item produced by a modest firm upset its record. So Dearborn decided to freeze out K-P, and notified its distributors. The campaign was effective, and as a result, K-P couldn't sell any jacks directly to Dearborn dealers or distributors. K-P finally agreed to terms. But when Dearborn returned its purchase order, it included objections to some of the conditions, and negotiations were once again at a stalemate.

This time it appears that Dearborn was the first to blink. On November 5, 1947, a compromise was reached. Dearborn then placed an order for 19,000 jacks and a material commitment for an additional 24,000 jacks.

As a sidelight, Poor and associates in 1948 canceled their Dearborn dealer franchise, citing Hudson's objections to having its cars displayed and sold alongside Ford products. In addition, they informed Dearborn they intended to resume selling the old-style jacks to Ferguson. And they had recently developed a jack for the John Deere tractor with hydraulic lift.

Dearborn didn't object, perhaps because it had reviewed the sales data for 1947 that indicated overall tractor and implement sales totaled $12,000,000. Of that amount, only $12,000 was tractor jack sales. There was an increase in revenue from jack sales in 1948, but this was still insignificant compared to overall sales.

Thanks to the great jack caper, and with all the jacks out there, you have to wonder whether the tractors spent more time in the air or in the field.

The angle of this solidly built later Ferguson terracer blade could be varied almost infinitely from left to right. And thanks to its trailing tail wheel, it could also be used in a pinch as a land plane for leveling fields.

This extremely early Ferguson terracer blade doesn't have a tail wheel. It's angle of attack can be adjusted into any of nine different angles from left to right.

Cordwood Saw

Procurement of the cordwood saw proved as straightforward as that of the jack had proved complex. Sales numbers of the saws didn't approach those of other implements and attachments, because the cordwood saw was both a seasonal and a regional item.

Dellinger Manufacturing Company, Lancaster, Pennsylvania, began as a general repair shop in 1895. It eventually began making farm implements for the local market. By 1932, it had a small distribution network and was marketing, among other things, corn shellers and huskers, land rollers, ensilage cutters, feed mixers, and stationary and tractor-attached cordwood saws. The company was owned by Paul Dellinger, who served as president, while Myles Sensinig was company engineer. Shortly after seeing their first 9N, Dellinger and Sensinig designed a three-point mounted cordwood saw to fit the tractor, and its patent was in the name of both men.

As with many other implements modified for the 9N, the Dellinger cordwood saw found its way to Ferguson distributors probably as early as 1940. Ferguson distributors were also handling another cordwood saw that was manufactured by the Turner Manufacturing Company, Statesville, North Carolina. Possibly a deciding factor that led Ferguson to eventually choose Dellinger as a saw supplier was that Dellinger held a comparatively high WPB quota for saws during the war years.

Early in 1942 Ferguson approached Dellinger for distribution rights for the saw. Documents suggest that Dellinger responded favorably to Dearborn's first inquiry seeking a supply of saws. The negotiations with Ferguson were simple. The contract, in part, stipulated that Ferguson would buy its cordwood saws from Dellinger, and Dellinger would grant Ferguson exclusive rights to sales of the saws.

Dellinger manufactured the basic implement framework and went to outside suppliers for component parts such as castings, bearings, springs, bolts, and saw blades. Interestingly enough, saw blades were in such short supply, just like disc blades, that some saws were shipped without blades.

From 1942 through 1946, Ferguson purchased 25,000 cordwood saws from Dellinger

This early Ferguson blade was manufactured by the Carrington Terracer Company, Fulton, Missouri. It carries a Harry Ferguson, Inc., Detroit, Michigan, identification plate, too. The blade is a Type BF-FO-20.

before the general cutback initiated by Ferguson in the last half of 1946. Delivery of saws to Dearborn began in the fall of 1947 at a rate of 750 per month.

During these years, Ferguson engineers had designed and patented the company's own saw. Nobody today knows what design novelties it claimed and whether or not it reached production. It's believed that Dellinger supplied both Ferguson and Dearborn with saws that were identical except for the color and nameplate. In fact, much like the mower and cultivator, the first sample saw for the Dearborn's May distributor meeting was disassembled, repainted Dearborn red, reassembled, and then shipped to the meeting. Apparently "red" sold well, because during the last six months of 1947, Dearborn bought 6,686 cordwood saws from Dellinger.

The Arps Corporation also made a cordwood saw, but it never did well.

Almost certainly manufactured by the Arps Corporation as its "Blackhawk" snowplow, this is the photograph Ford used to promote the snowplow attachment.

Probably the most intriguing of all three-point attachments is the Dearborn tractor jack that raises all four wheels off the ground a couple of inches. It was designed to be a quicker and easier way to change the spacing of the wheels for various crops or to change any single tire. The tractor isn't driven onto the jack. Instead, the jack pieces are positioned under the tractor's rear-end housing and under the oil pan. When the hydraulic touch control is raised, the tractor just rolls on up on the supports.

Ford Suppliers As of April 1946

Photographs of the Ferguson dirt scoop were used in various advertising and promotion materials.

Alexander Manufacturing Company, Picayune, Mississippi: *Disc harrow, bush and bog*

American Road Equipment Company Inc., Omaha, Nebraska: *Loader, front-end*

Arps Corporation, New Holstein, Wisconsin: *Universal frame, angledozer blade snowplow, blade-type snowplow, V-type utility blade, scoop lift-type*

David Bradley, Inc., Bradley, Illinois: *Shares, solid and soft center*

The Budd Company, Detroit, Michigan: *Plow moldboard*

A. S. Campbell Company, East Boston, Massachusetts: *Wagon, four-wheel*

M. A. Case Manufacturing Company, Mt. Clemens, Michigan: *Weed hook, swinging drawbar*

Continental Farm Equipment Company, Omaha, Nebraska: *Disc harrow, single lift-type*

Danuser Machine Company, Fulton, Missouri: *Blade, all-purpose; post hole digger*

Dellinger Manufacturing Company, Lancaster, Pennsylvania: *Saw, cordwood*

Dempster Mill Manufacturing Company, Beatrice, Nebraska: *Planter, lister, cultivator*

Detroit Harvester Company, Detroit, Michigan: *Mower, agricultural, and mower, heavy duty*

Empire Plow Company, Cleveland, Ohio: *Stabilizer kits*

Farm Rite Implement Company, Chicago, Illinois: *Disc harrow, tandem; weeder*

Farm Tools, Inc., Evansville, Indiana: *Disc harrow, tandem; spring-tooth harrow; rotary hoe; plow bases, slat and two-way*

Ford Motor Company, Detroit, Michigan: *Tractor, PTO, and pulley assembly*

French & Hecht, Inc., Davenport, Iowa: *Wagon, standard; coulter; two-way plow*

K-P Manufacturing Company, Olathe, Kansas: *Jack, tractor*

G. A. Kelly Plow Company, Longview, Texas: *Middlebuster base; planter; middlebuster attachment; fertilizer distributor attachment*

Parker Plow Company, Richmond, Michigan: *Soil pulverizer; plow bases and shares, chilled cast*

Phillips Foundry Company, Bakersfield, California: *Plow, two-way*

Pittsburgh Forgings Company, Coraopolis, Pennsylvania: *Cultivator, rigid shank; cultivator, spring shank; cultivator, field; middlebuster*

Southern Iron & Equipment Company, Atlanta, Georgia: *Plow disc*

Superior Pipe Specialties Company, Chicago, Illinois: *Loader, heavy-duty; loader, material bucket; loader, manure fork*

Towner Manufacturing Company, Santa Ana, California: *West Coast Implements: Subsoiler; ridger, disc; disc harrow, offset; spring-tooth harrow; depth roller; chisel, light-duty; chisel, heavy-duty; cultivator, spring shank; cultivator, coil shank; spring shank furrower; vegetable lifter; trip dump scraper; buck scraper; land leveler; tool bars; tractor hitches*

Tractor Appliance Company, Minneapolis, Minnesota: *Cultivator, front-end*

A. F. Wagner Iron Works, Milwaukee, Wisconsin: *Loader, heavy-duty; loader, material bucket; loader, manure fork; loader, crane attachment*

Western Land Roller Company, Hastings, Nebraska: *Sweep rake*

Wood Brothers, Inc., Des Moines, Iowa: *Corn picker*

The three-point hitch arrangement stimulated some farmers to build their own attachments for assistance in doing various job. A case in point is this platform readily made from a few pieces of angle iron and 1-inch-thick pieces of lumber. It's handy for hauling a sack of feed or piling on wood or . . .

The Wood Brothers

Any work concerning Ford-Ferguson implements wouldn't be complete without mentioning the Wood Brothers Thresher Company. Franz John Wood and his brother, R. L., founded the Wood Brothers Thresher Company in 1893 at Rushford, Minnesota. In 1899, they moved the company, by now known as Wood Brothers, to Des Moines, Iowa.

Before the Ford-Ferguson split, Belle City Manufacturing Company, Inc., Racine, Wisconsin, supplied the tractor manufacturer with the corn pickers that were sold. Afterward, Wood Brothers, Inc., provided corn pickers for Dearborn, while Belle City continued making corn pickers for Ferguson.

In 1953, the company was sold to Dearborn Motors of Detroit. In 1955, the Wood Brothers plant became the Des Moines implement plant of the Ford Motor Company. After Ford bought the company, the switch was made from the Continental Red Field engine that the Wood Brothers had been using as power units to the same engine as delivered in the N-Series Ford tractor. There was only a minor difference in the block.

Harold Brock was certainly correct when he said the industry got involved. Companies sprang up to meet the implement demands of the Ford N-Series tractors. Many inventors and entrepreneurs produced a long line of implements and accessories for the N-Series tractors besides those marketed through Ferguson and/or Dearborn.

Danuser Machine Company, Fulton, Missouri, has always been a key player in the three-point attachment earthmoving equipment business.

Implements Sold per N-Series Tractor

T his information shows the average number of implements sold per N-Series tractor and is from a 1946 report on Harry Ferguson, Inc., conducted by the firm of McKinsey, Kearney & Company of Chicago, Illinois. This report also states that Harry Ferguson, Inc., had set sales goals of 10 implements for every tractor. While some dealers had reached this goal, McKinsey, Kearney & Company felt that six implements per tractor would be a more realistic figure.

1939	1.02
1940	1.34
1941	1.97
1942	2.97
1943	2.61
1944	3.83
1945	5.82
1946	3.84

This beautifully restored Dearborn cordwood saw is powered by a belt pulley mounted on the tractor PTO. Extra pulley shown is attached to PTO.

There are some slight variations between this Dearborn cordwood saw and the other two pictured in this chapter.

This Dearborn crane has many uses. Two popular tasks it's often asked to handle are picking up and carrying heavy items to a new location and pulling up fence posts. The amount of leverage applied can be varied depending on which of the three hooks are used.

The story of the three-point system doesn't end here. After Ferguson parted company with Ford, the line continued to expand and flourish. Ferguson imported in excess of 25,000 English-manufactured tractors in 1947–1948. Many of the initial equipment suppliers continued manufacturing implements for Ferguson to market with the English tractors.

Also, the Ferguson Park plant in Detroit, Michigan, was in production by October 1948. It allowed Ferguson to continue to be a vital domestic farm machinery source.

In 1953, Harry Ferguson, Inc., merged with Massey-Harris of Canada. Today, Massey-Ferguson is a global enterprise providing state-of-the-art farm machinery worldwide.

The Dearborn line continued to expand until 1955. At that time it became part of the Ford Motor Company, with tractors and implements sold under the Ford name. It, too, continues to be a farm machinery name recognized wherever there are farmers in the world.

This continually expanding "list" of farm implements designed for the three-point system certainly gives conclusive testimony of man's desire to seek out a "better way."

This Dearborn subsoiler is built strongly enough to withstand the strain of being socked into the ground deeply enough to break up hardpan.

The Ferguson subsoiler differs from the Dearborn subsoiler in angle and width of blade and in utilizing a spring.

Below: "Jack-of-all-trades" is an apt label for this English Ferguson Transport Box. It was originally designed to allow a dairyman to haul six milk cans from dairy to nearby creamery. However, it's also handy for carrying wood, rocks, coal, or whatever needs hauling.

Ferguson in the mid-1950s designed and built a semimounted forage harvester and a semimounted baler, both of which were partially three-point-mounted. This is the power source for both. The reason this power unit exists is that the tractor doesn't have enough power to run the equipment while also pulling the equipment and a wagon. Set up on this factory three-point hitch arrangement, the power unit can be easily moved for use with a feed grinder or sawmill. It puts out approximately 40 horsepower. Note the PTO and pulley at left.

A three-point hitch bracket working off the lift arms with a kind of grapple hook engages a ring on the tongue of this Ferguson manure spreader. By raising the three-point lift arms, the hook goes down and under, then up and into the "eye" of the tongue end of the spreader. The spreader control can be reached from the tractor seat so the operator never has to leave the seat to make changes.

Right: Ferguson had this low-volume sprayer made by another manufacturer in England. It's a one-of-a-kind in the United States.

Left: One of the largest pieces of equipment to be hooked up via the three-point system is this English-built Ferguson hammer mill. It's a Type H-LE-20. To find such a hammer mill in such good condition is a rarity, because most of those remaining in the United Kingdom have rusted out, due to wet and salty conditions. Owned by David Lory, this is the only one in the United States.

This Type U-UE-20 is an English-built winch. It was built for Ferguson by C. M. Hesford, Ltd. The winch weighs 600 pounds. It carries a 40-foot-long cable rated at 7,000 pounds pull. This is the only such piece of equipment in the United States.

Probably made in 1940 or 1941 in England for Ferguson, this trailer features a 4,000-pound hydraulic dump, three-cylinder, telescoping hydraulic hoist that connects to Ferguson linkage system. The maximum tilt angle is 55 degrees, and the telescoping top link in compression safely transfers part of the load to the tractor. The telescoping action also allows for various irregularities when traveling over uneven ground. It has a 51-cubic-foot capacity. The sales literature of the period advises that due to the restrictions of World War II, no more will be produced. The trailer brake is from a Model T Ford truck. This handbrake is positioned so the driver can easily turn around in his seat to work it.

Ferguson Supplies, 1939-1948

(May not include all suppliers)

Alexander Manufacturing Company, Picayune, Mississippi: *Disc harrow, bush and bog*

Arps Corporation, New Holstein, Wisconsin: *Universal frame; angledozer blade; snowplow, blade-type; snowplow, V-type; utility blade; scoop, lift-type*

David Bradley, Inc., Bradley, Illinois: *Shares, solid and soft center; rear-mounted mowers*

The Budd Company, Detroit, Michigan: *Moldboard plows*

A. S. Campbell Company, East Boston, Massachusetts: *Wagon, four-wheel*

Carrington Terracer Company, Fulton, Missouri: *Disc terracer; grader blade*

M. S. Case Manufacturing Company, Mt. Clemens, Michigan: *Weed hook; swinging drawbar; fertilizer attachment*

Continental Farm Equipment Company, Omaha, Nebraska: *Disc harrow, single lift-type*

Danuser Machine Company, Fulton, Missouri: *Blade, all-purpose; posthole digger*

Dellinger Manufacturing Company, Lancaster, Pennsylvania: *Cordwood saw*

Dempster Mill Manufacturing Company, Beatrice, Nebraska: *Planter; lister cultivators; grain drills*

Detroit Harvester Company, Detroit, Michigan: *Mower, side-mounted; mower, rear-mounted*

Empire Plow Company, Cleveland, Ohio: *Rigid-shank cultivators; spring-shank cultivators; tillers; middlebusters; ridgers; implement service parts*

Farm Rite Implement Company, Chicago, Illinois: *Disc harrow, tandem; seeder; spring-tooth harrows; rear-mount mowers*

Farm Tools, Inc., Evansville, Indiana: *Disc harrow, tandem; single lift-type disc harrow; spring-tooth harrow; spike-tooth harrow; rotary hoe; plow bases, slat and two-way*

Ford Motor Company, Detroit, Michigan: *Tractor; PTO; pulley assembly; plows; middlebuster; cultivator parts*

French & Hecht, Inc., Davenport, Iowa: *Coulter; two-way plow; furrow wheel assembly*

K-P Manufacturing Company, Olathe, Kansas: *Jack, tractor*

G. A. Kelly Plow Company, Longview, Texas: *Middlebuster base; planter; middlebuster attachment; fertilizer distributor attachment; disc terracer*

Lynchburg Plow Works, Richmond, Michigan: *Plowshares*

Parker Plow Company, Richmond, Michigan: *Soil pulverizer; plow bases and shares, chilled cast*

Pittsburgh Forgings Company, Coraopolis, Pennsylvania: *Cultivator, rigid-shank; cultivator, spring-shank; field middlebuster*

Standard Steel Company, Kansas City, Missouri: *Corn planters*

Superior Pipe Specialties Company, Chicago, Illinois: *Loader, heavy-duty; loader, material bucket; loader, manure fork*

Towner Manufacturing Company, Santa Ana, California: *West Coast Implements: Subsoiler; ridger disc; disc harrow, offset; spring-tooth harrow; depth roller; chisel, light-duty; chisel, heavy-duty; cultivator, spring-shank; cultivator, coil-shank; spring-shank furrower; vegetable lifter; loader, front-end; trip dump scraper; buck scraper; land leveler; tool bars; tractor hitches*

Tractor Appliance Company, Minneapolis, Minnesota: *Cultivator shanks and shovels*

A. F. Wagner Iron Works, Milwaukee, Wisconsin: *Loader, heavy-duty; loader, material bucket; loader, manure fork; loader, crane attachment*

Western Land Roller Company, Hastings, Nebraska: *Sweep rake*

Wood Brothers, Inc., Des Moines, Iowa: *Corn picker, combine*

Thanks to its hydraulic system, the Ferguson tractor could not only tow this two-wheel trailer, but also allow the farmer to empty it without being forced to resort to a scoop shovel.

This driver and breaker were made by Danuser Machine Company for setting both wood and steel posts.

Hitches and Tool Bars

Ferguson Types

Description	Type No.
Towner heavy-duty utility hitch complete	UF-I
Towner tool bar, 2 inch square, 24 inch long	U-100
30-inch long	U-101
42-inch long	U-102
48-inch long	U-103
54-inch long	U-104
60-inch long	U-105
66-inch long	U-106
72-inch long	U-107
78-inch long	U-108
84-inch long	U-109
90-inch long	U-110
96-inch long	U-111
108-inch long	U-112
120-inch long	U-113

Vegetable Lifter

Ferguson Types

Description	Type No.
Towner beet or vegetable lifter (with hitch, tool bar & standards)	U-1 106-B
Less hitch & tool bar	F-106-B
Coulter Brackets (pair)	F-106-B-CB

Spreaders

Ferguson Types

Description	Type No.
Manure spreader 48-bushel box 7.50x16 6-ply tires	A-JO-20
Manure spreader with Ferguson hitch, 7.50x16 6-ply tires	A-JO-21
With conventional draw bar hitch and crank-type stand, 7.50x16 6-ply tires	A-JO-22
With universal hitch	A-JO-62

Dearborn/Ford Models
N/A

Wagons

Ferguson Types

Description	Type No.
Tractor-wagon, 6x16 tires extra	W-JO-20

Dearborn/Ford Models

Description	ID No.
Dearborn farm wagon	21-2

Cranes

Ferguson Types

Description	Type No.
Rear crane for 9N and 2N model tractors	C-UO-20
For TE or TO model tractors	C-UO-21

Dearborn/Ford models
N/A

Grinder

Ferguson Types

Description	Type No.
W. W. Triplet grinder equipped with 16 stellite-faced hammers and one 3/8-inch size screen. (No flat Drive Belt is furnished.)	WW-2-G

Extra Equipment:

Description	Type No.
Screen in sizes from 1/8-inch to 2-inch openings stellite-surfaced 2 1/2-inch diameter knives	T-33-X

Dearborn/Ford models
N/A

Corn Pickers/Harvesters

Ferguson types

Description	Type No.
Corn picker: One row with husker, manual control tilt lever	EH
Corn picker: One row with husker, hydraulic lift equipped	EH-II
Corn picker: One row with snapper	ES
Hydraulic lift kit for installation on all model EH or ES pickers	P-HO-61
Blower unit kit for installation on the 1950 model FH or EH-H picker	P-HO-63
Blower unit kit for installation on 1948, 1949 model picker	N/A
Mild husking roll discs	P-6378-AR
Packages of 50 mild snapping rolls	PHO-60
Mud scrapers, two scrapers per kit	P-6478-AR

Dearborn/Ford Models

Description	ID No.
Dearborn-Wood Brothers pull-type, single row, PTO	16-4
Ford one row mounted corn picker (for 9N, 8N, 600, 700, 800 & 900 tractors)	16-65
Ford two row mounted corn harvester (for 9N, 8N, NAA, 600-900 tractors)	16-66
Ford two row mounted corn harvester (for 700 & 900 tractors)	16-76

Combines

Ferguson Types

Description	Type No.
Wood Brothers combine, pull-type 60-inch header	5F
Wood Brothers combine, pull-type 84-inch header	7F
Wood Brothers combine, pull-type 72-inch header, PTO or auxiliary Wisconsin engine	WB-6-C

Dearborn/Ford models

Description	ID No.
Wood Bros. pull-type combine, 5-feet header (built 1937–1942)	5F
Wood Bros. pull-type combine, 6-feet header (built 1943–1945)	6F
Wood Bros. pull-type combine, 7-feet header (built 1937–1942)	7F

Road Maintainer

Dearborn Models

Description	ID No.
For mounting on 8N tractor	L19-35
Berm leveler attachment for road maintainer	L19-36

Bibliography

American Farm Tools from Hand-Power to Steam-Power. Hurt, R. Douglas. Manhattan, Kansas: Sunflower University Press, 1982.

Avery Steam Traction Engines and Attachments. Peoria, Illinois. Avery Company Manufacturers. 1914.

Case Machinery. Racine, Wisconsin. J. I. Case Threshing Machine Company Inc. 1918.

Farm Tools through the Ages. Partridge, Michael. Boston, Massachusetts: Promontory Press.

Ferguson Implements and Accessories. Farnworth, John. Alexandria Bay, New York: Farming Press, 1996.

Ferguson—A Brief History of His Life and Tractors. Baber, John, and George Field. Harry Coventry, United Kingdom: Massey-Ferguson Tractors Limited, 1993.

Harry Ferguson. Martin, Bill. Belfast, Ireland. Ulster Folk & Transport Museum.

Harry Ferguson—A Tribute. United Kingdom: Royal Norfolk Agricultural Society, 1994.

The New Ferguson Album. Booth, Colin E., and Condie, Allan T. United Kingdom. Allan T. Condie Publications, 1986.

Tools for Agriculture. United Kingdom: Intermediate Technology Publications Ltd.

Tractor Pioneer: The Life of Harry Ferguson. Fraser, Colin. Athens, Ohio: Ohio University Press, 1973.

Index

Index